CAMBRIDGE

Official Cambridge Exam Preparation

CB082021

B2 FIRST FOR SCHOOLS 4

WITH ANSWERS

AUTHENTIC PRACTICE TESTS

WITH AUDIO

WITH RESOURCE BANK

Cambridge University Press
www.cambridge.org/elt

Cambridge Assessment English
www.cambridgeenglish.org

Information on this title: www.cambridge.org/9781108780100

© Cambridge University Press and Cambridge Assessment 2021

It is normally necessary for written permission for copying to be obtained *in advance* from a publisher. The sample answer sheets at the back of this book are designed to be copied and distributed in class.
The normal requirements are waived here and it is not necessary to write to Cambridge University Press for permission for an individual teacher to make copies for use within his or her own classroom. Only those pages that carry the wording '© Cambridge Assessment 2021 Photocopiable' may be copied.

First published 2021

20 19 18 17 16 15 14 13 12 11 10 9 8 7 6 5 4 3 2 1

Printed in Malaysia by Vivar Printing

A catalogue record for this publication is available from the British Library

ISBN 978-1-108-78010-0 B2 First for Schools 4 Student's Book with Answers with Audio with Resource Bank
ISBN 978-1-108-74805-6 B2 First for Schools 4 Student's Book without answers

The publishers have no responsibility for the persistence or accuracy of URLs for external or third-party internet websites referred to in this publication, and do not guarantee that any content on such websites is, or will remain, accurate or appropriate. Information regarding prices, travel timetables and other factual information given in this work is correct at the time of first printing but the publishers do not guarantee the accuracy of such information thereafter.

Contents

Introduction

Prepare for the exam with practice tests from Cambridge

Inside you'll find four authentic examination papers from Cambridge Assessment English. They are the perfect way to practise – EXACTLY like the real exam.

Why are they unique?

All our authentic practice tests go through the same design process as the *B2 First for Schools* exam. We check every single part of our practice tests with real students under exam conditions, to make sure we give you the most authentic experience possible.

Students can practise these tests on their own or with the help of a teacher to familiarise themselves with the exam format, understand the scoring system and practise exam technique.

Cambridge English Qualifications	CEFR Level	UK National Qualifications
C2 Proficiency	C2	3
C1 Advanced	C1	2
B2 First for Schools	B2	1
B1 Preliminary for Schools	B1	Entry 3
A2 Key for Schools	A2	Entry 2

Further information

The information contained in this practice book is designed to be an overview of the exam. For a full description of all of the above exams, including information about task types, testing focus and preparation, please see the relevant handbooks, which can be obtained from the Cambridge Assessment English website at: **cambridgeenglish.org**.

The structure of *B2 First for Schools*: an overview

The *Cambridge English Qualifications B2 First for Schools* examination consists of four papers:

Reading and Use of English: 1 hour 15 minutes
Candidates need to be able to understand texts from publications such as fiction and non-fiction books, journals, newspapers and magazines.

Writing: 1 hour 20 minutes
Candidates have to show that they can produce two different pieces of writing: a compulsory essay in Part 1 and one from a choice of four tasks in Part 2. Question 5 in Part 2 is based on a set reading text. These practice tests do not include this task as the set text changes every two years. You can find more information about the set text at the Cambridge English website (see page 4 for details).

Listening: 40 minutes approximately
Candidates need to show they can understand the meaning of a range of spoken material, including lectures, radio broadcasts, speeches and talks.

Speaking: 14 minutes (or 20 minutes for groups of 3)
Candidates take the Speaking test with another candidate or in a group of three, and are tested on their ability to take part in different types of interaction: with the examiner, with the other candidate and by themselves.

	Overall length	Number of tasks/parts	Number of items
Reading and Use of English	1 hour and 15 minutes	7	52
Writing	1 hour and 20 minutes	2	-
Listening	approx. 40 mins	4	30
Speaking	14 mins	4	-
Total	3 hours and 29 mins approximately		

Grading

All candidates receive a Statement of Results and candidates whose performance ranges between CEFR Levels B1 and C1 (Cambridge English Scale scores of 140–190) also receive a certificate.

- Candidates who achieve **Grade A** (Cambridge English Scale scores of 180–190) receive the B2 First Certificate in English stating that they demonstrated ability at Level C1.
- Candidates who achieve **Grade B** or **C** (Cambridge English Scale scores of 160–179) receive the B2 First Certificate in English at Level B2.
- Candidates whose performance is below B2 level, but falls within **Level B1** (Cambridge English Scale scores of 140–159), receive a Cambridge English certificate stating that they have demonstrated ability at Level B1.

For further information on grading and results, go to the website (see page 4 for details).

Speaking: an overview for candidates

You take the Speaking test with another candidate (possibly two candidates), referred to here as your partner. There are two examiners. One will speak to you and your partner and the other will be listening. Both examiners will award marks.

Part 1 (2 minutes)

The examiner asks you and your partner questions about yourselves. You may be asked about things like 'your home town', 'your interests', 'your career plans', etc.

Part 2 (4 minutes)

The examiner gives you two photographs and asks you to talk about them for one minute. The examiner then asks your partner a question about your photographs and your partner responds briefly.

Then the examiner gives your partner two different photographs. Your partner talks about these photographs for one minute. This time the examiner asks you a question about your partner's photographs and you respond briefly.

Part 3 (4 minutes)

The examiner asks you and your partner to talk together for 2 minutes. They give you a task to look at so you can think about and discuss an idea, giving reasons for your opinion. For example, you may be asked to think about some changes in the world, or about spending free time with your family.

After you have discussed the task for about two minutes with your partner, the examiner will ask you a follow-up question, which you should discuss for a further minute.

Part 4 (4 minutes)

The examiner asks some further questions related to your topic from Part 3. You may comment on your partner's answers if you wish.

Test 1

READING AND USE OF ENGLISH (1 hour 15 minutes)

Part 1

For questions **1–8**, read the text below and decide which answer (**A**, **B**, **C** or **D**) best fits each gap. There is an example at the beginning (**0**).

Mark your answers on the separate answer sheet.

Example:

0 **A** choice **B** variety **C** diversity **D** selection

0	A o	B ●	C o	D o

Building roads with waste coffee

Used coffee grounds, which are left in coffee machines after cups of coffee have been made, are already recycled in a **(0)** .... of ways. Now a team of scientists have discovered that they can also be **(1)** .... to good use as a material for building roads.

Coffee lover and professor of geotechnical engineering Arul Arulrajah **(2)** .... the idea of using them in this way after observing workers at his favourite coffee shops in Melbourne, Australia, **(3)** .... throwing away used coffee grounds. He then **(4)** .... several experiments to find something suitable to mix with the coffee grounds to **(5)** .... the base layer under a road's **(6)** ....

According to Professor Arulrajah's estimates, the 150 kg of coffee grounds the team **(7)** .... from Melbourne's coffee houses every week could create enough material to build about five kilometres of road per year. This would **(8)** .... to a reduction in the amount of organic and industrial waste that ends up in the city's landfills.

1	**A**	made	**B**	put	**C**	given	**D**	got
2	**A**	considered	**B**	regarded	**C**	acknowledged	**D**	realised
3	**A**	forgetfully	**B**	carelessly	**C**	neglectfully	**D**	insensitively
4	**A**	controlled	**B**	directed	**C**	guided	**D**	conducted
5	**A**	compose	**B**	form	**C**	position	**D**	install
6	**A**	covering	**B**	ground	**C**	surface	**D**	exterior
7	**A**	collects	**B**	keeps	**C**	saves	**D**	stores
8	**A**	bring	**B**	come	**C**	lead	**D**	arrive

→ p. 109

Part 2

For questions **9–16**, read the text below and think of the word which best fits each gap. Use only **one** word in each gap. There is an example at the beginning (**0**).

Write your answers **IN CAPITAL LETTERS on the separate answer sheet.**

Example: | 0 | *W H A T* |

The amazing Atacama Desert

When you think of a desert, **(0)** .... first comes to mind? Is it a hot, dry and empty landscape? For the Atacama Desert in Chile, that image is only partly true. It is actually pretty cold, with daily temperatures ranging **(9)** .... 0 to 25 degrees centigrade. But **(10)** .... is certainly no doubt that the Atacama Desert is dry. Despite **(11)** .... located right next to the Pacific Ocean, it's actually the world's driest desert, some parts of which have not had any rainfall for over 400 years. So it may come **(12)** .... a surprise to learn that it does actually rain in this desert. Every five to seven years **(13)** .... average, heavy rainfall soaks the landscape and then, all **(14)** .... a sudden, something magical happens: the desert is transformed into a carpet of colourful flowers. This incredible sight lasts for just a **(15)** .... short weeks and attracts thousands of visitors, eager **(16)** .... enjoy such a rare occurrence.

 → p. 109

Part 3

For questions **17–24**, read the text below. Use the word given in capitals at the end of some of the lines to form a word that fits in the gap **in the same line**. There is an example at the beginning **(0)**.

Write your answers **IN CAPITAL LETTERS on the separate answer sheet.**

Example: | **0** | S C I E N T I F I C |

Important helium gas discovery

Helium is a gas which is very important for the running of major	
(0) .... facilities. It is also used in medical equipment like	**SCIENCE**
brain scanners. People use it for their **(17)** .... too, filling party	**AMUSE**
balloons with it so they float in the air.	
It is found **(18)** .... inside rocks, and until recently, helium was	**GROUND**
only ever discovered **(19)** .... and in small quantities. There	**ACCIDENT**
was such **(20)** .... among doctors over the steady decline in	**ANXIOUS**
reserves that they called for a ban on its use in party balloons in order to	
help prevent a global **(21)** .... of the precious gas.	**SHORT**
The discovery of a vast reserve of helium in east Africa in 2016, therefore,	
came as a great **(22)** .... The store of helium found contains	**RELIEVE**
approximately 1.5 billion litres of the gas, **(23)** .... have said.	**RESEARCH**
A team from the UK and Norway made this significant find after applying	
techniques normally used in the **(24)** .... of oil and gas.	**EXPLORE**

→ p. 109

Part 4

For questions **25–30**, complete the second sentence so that it has a similar meaning to the first sentence, using the word given. **Do not change the word given.** You must use between **two** and **five** words, including the word given. Here is an example (**0**).

Example:

0 Prizes are given out when the school year finishes.

PLACE

Prize-giving .... end of the school year.

The gap can be filled by the words 'takes place at the', so you write:

Example:	**0**	*TAKES PLACE AT THE*

Write **only** the missing words **IN CAPITAL LETTERS on the separate answer sheet.**

---

25 Because Alice was finding her book very interesting, she didn't hear the doorbell ring.

ABSORBED

Alice was .... her book that she didn't hear the doorbell ring.

26 We missed the train because we didn't leave home early enough.

IF

We wouldn't have missed the train .... home early enough.

27 I'm sure Diane can solve this maths puzzle.

CAPABLE

I'm sure Diane .... this maths puzzle.

28 I'll lend you my bike, but only if you look after it.

LONG

I'll lend you my bike .... care of it.

29 'I don't want to help you with your homework, Sam,' said his sister.

WILLING

Sam's sister said she .... him with his homework.

30 'I'm not going to miss my best friend's party!' Mary told her mother.

DETERMINED

Mary told her mother that she .... to her best friend's party.

→ p. 109

Part 5

You are going to read a magazine article about a teenager called Harry Dean who went on a freestyle ski jumping course. For questions **31–36**, choose the answer (**A**, **B**, **C** or **D**) which you think fits best according to the text.

Mark your answers on the separate answer sheet.

Learning freestyle ski jumping

by Harry Dean

'Remember, speed is your friend, not your enemy,' said Gareth, our instructor, as we looked down the ski slope. 'Now, who wants to go first?' The assembled group looked nervous. Then one guy, David, who'd had some experience of freestyle ski-jumping, and presumably wanted to preserve his reputation as someone who knew exactly what he was doing, pushed forward, skiing off down the slope towards the jump. He hit the approach ramp fast and flew upwards, arms flailing in the air. Even to our untutored eyes, something was wrong. We held our breath. He hit the ground, losing both skis, and flipped head-first into the snow. 'Remember,' Gareth then kindly informed us, 'speed is an unpredictable beast.'

Perhaps I just wasn't cut out for this freestyle stuff. On previous skiing holidays, I'd enjoyed messing about, practising turns in the snow. I just wasn't one of those teenagers who spent their time doing freestyle tricks on ramps and half pipes in skateboard parks. Deep down, I'd always thought it looked fun, but reckoned that, with my lack of know-how, if I'd tried to join with the skateboarders, with their baggy trousers and special language, I'd have risked total ridicule.

Then my parents decided we'd have a winter holiday at a training centre for freestyle skiing in the USA. It had a huge indoor facility near the slopes, with trampolines, and ski jumps covered in artificial snow, from which students leapt, shrieking as they attempted their new tricks, then landed in pits of foam cubes. After practising their moves indoors, students headed outside. 'Progression is inevitable!' the centre's slogan cheerily assured us. 'Before places like this trained people up, inexperienced ski jumpers would just throw themselves down the slopes and hope for the best,' said Gareth. 'But remember – once you're on the real jumps, if you hit the knuckle, you'll be in trouble.'

The 'knuckle' Gareth was referring to is the flat section behind the jump before the slope steepens again to become the landing zone proper. Land in the zone and your motion continues forward, minimising impact. Land on the flat and you stop dead, which is painful. Hence the need for speed. At first, though, it was all but impossible to convince my body to ignore what my brain was screaming at me and to race straight towards the jump. My legs would virtually go into reverse as I neared the launch point, so I came slamming down onto the knuckle. I managed not to fall, but by midday I felt several centimetres shorter. 'You need to control the jump, not let it control you,' said Gareth.

Day two started on the trampolines in the centre. I'd expected to hate being stuck indoors, looking at the snowy peaks outside, but bouncing on the trampolines was addictive. Some of the drills copied moves we'd make while ski-jumping, others were aimed at teaching 'aerial awareness' – knowing what your body was doing as you spun in space. Gareth gave us a running commentary. My 'aerial awareness' apparently needed work – and it's true that, every time I tried, I was aware of the moment before take-off, and nothing more until I found myself lying in the foam cubes next to the trampoline.

We moved back to the mountain to try again. Inevitably, there were more setbacks before I finally landed properly. Gareth seemed as delighted as me, and for a few moments I was walking on air, with the sheer pride of having achieved such an elusive goal. But that was short-lived. On the final run of the day, I forced myself not to reduce speed as I approached the jump, became airborne, and came down appropriately in the landing zone. Then I noticed both skis sliding down the slope ahead, no longer attached to my feet.

31 Harry suggests that David

A had thought he would be in a more advanced group.
B was a good role-model for beginners in the group.
C had not listened to the teacher's instructions.
D was not as skilled as he appeared to believe.

32 What is meant by 'flailing in the air' in line 10?

A announcing his arrival
B suitably positioned for jumping
C waving around uselessly
D raised high in victory

33 What does Harry say about his experience of freestyle sports?

A His fear of failure prevented him from participating.
B His natural ability was never fully recognised.
C He discovered that his original opinion of freestylers was justified.
D He regrets not having developed the skills necessary to do well.

34 During Harry's first attempts at ski jumping, he

A felt inhibited by the warning he had been given.
B struggled to overcome his natural instincts.
C showed a determination to improve his technique.
D regarded the fact that he remained upright as progress.

35 While training on the trampoline, Harry

A resented the fact that he had to stay indoors.
B wished he had realised how difficult he would find it.
C failed to see the relevance of what he was asked to do.
D felt that the criticism he received was fair.

36 When Harry returned to the slopes after his indoor training, he

A managed several surprisingly competent jumps.
B became convinced perfect jumps were impossible to achieve.
C got into difficulty after managing a good jump.
D suffered a loss of confidence before his last jump.

→ p. 109

Part 6

You are going to read a magazine article about a painting created by a computer. Six sentences have been removed from the article. Choose from the sentences **A–G** the one which fits each gap (**37–42**). There is one extra sentence which you do not need to use.

Mark your answers on the separate answer sheet.

A computer-generated painting

Born in Amsterdam in 1606, Rembrandt Harmenszoon van Rijn is one of the world's most renowned artists. The prolific painter was famous for his portraits and was admired for his ability to capture realistic emotions. Unfortunately, like many artists of his time, Rembrandt's talents were not recognised during his lifetime. The artist died penniless in 1669, after suffering many years of hardship.

Interestingly, a painting unveiled in Holland in 2016 has made headlines around the world because it looks as if it was painted by the famous 17th-century Dutch artist. **37** ______ It is, in fact, a brand new painting that uses technology to mimic his technique so perfectly that it could easily be mistaken for one created by the great artist himself.

The clever forgery, called the 'Next Rembrandt', took 18 months to complete and is the result of a collaboration between computer experts and art experts. The team collected data from the Dutch artist's 346 known paintings to help them imitate as closely as possible his technique, choice of colour, structure, texture and topic. They used facial recognition software and a unique computer programme to analyse the individual features of his style. **38** ______

The computer needed as much data as possible to enable it to mimic the artist's work accurately. Rembrandt painted a large number of portraits, many of which were of men with moustaches wearing black suits with white collars. **39** ______ They decided that the 'Next Rembrandt' would be a portrait of a white male between 30 and 40 years old, wearing black clothes, a white collar and a hat.

40 ______ The special software system that the team had designed gathered information about Rembrandt's style based on his use of geometry, the way he placed the objects and people in relation to one another in his paintings and his choice of paint colours. The data was used to generate the facial features for the 'Next Rembrandt'.

The individual elements were put together to form the face and the chest in the same proportions as the original paintings created by the Dutch artist. **41** ______ When this had been done, a 3D printer was used to bring the 'Next Rembrandt' to life. Comprising 148 million pixels and 13 layers of ultra-violet ink, the 'painting' is a clever forgery that looks exactly like an original Rembrandt, at least to the untrained eye.

The goal of the project was to start a discussion about how data and technology could become an essential part of the art world. The project was not universally popular, and did receive some criticism. **42** ______ Their aim was to ensure that the 'Next Rembrandt' would be a masterpiece, one that even the famous Dutch artist would be proud of, and they seem to have succeeded.

A However, many art historians, including Rembrandt experts, were incredibly supportive.

B Once the subject had been determined, the next stage of the process could begin.

C These included details like painting strokes, the artist's preferred angle and so on.

D As a result, they actually considered giving up on it at this point.

E The team then used technology to add depth and texture to their image.

F The authentic-looking masterpiece is not the work of Rembrandt, though.

G For this reason, the team settled on creating something similar.

→ p. 109

Part 7

You are going to read an article written by an architect about his work. For questions **43–52**, choose from the sections (**A–D**). The sections may be chosen more than once.

Mark your answers on the separate answer sheet.

In which section does the writer

warn that exercising may have the opposite effect to that intended?	**43**	
mention an increase in the size of something as the result of exercise?	**44**	
say even very gentle exercise can have a positive impact?	**45**	
explain why a comparison is a little misleading?	**46**	
give an example of an improvement in students' ability to focus?	**47**	
say what many people believed about the benefits of exercise has been proved correct?	**48**	
give advice on how to recall information more effectively?	**49**	
mention a doubt about why people sometimes experience a change of mood?	**50**	
warn that a particular type of exercise may not help with problem solving?	**51**	
welcome the idea of matching exercise type to particular mental challenges?	**52**	

 → p. 109

How physical exercise makes your brain work better

A The brain is often described as being 'like a muscle', however, this may not always be a helpful way of thinking about it. For example, if you want to improve the strength of your arms, you can exercise them and feel the results. When it comes to exercising your brain, this, of course, isn't possible. But it seems that by working your body's muscles you're actually benefitting your brain too. What's more, different physical activities can change the structure of your brain in different ways. As a result of research into how this happens, people will be able to select the form of exercise which best suits their needs – what to do if, for example, they want to perform well in a memory test – and this is good news. Researchers are still trying to work out why exercise seems to be so good for the brain. One possibility is that it increases blood flow. Exercise may also encourage the creation of new cells that are responsible for carrying messages between the brain and body. Until recently, few people thought this could happen in adult brains, but scientists now see this as a real possibility.

B It is well known that hard physical activity can have a positive effect on how you feel. For example, runners often get what's referred to as a 'runner's high' – that great feeling that follows intense exercise. Many people think this is due to endorphins, the chemicals in your bloodstream responsible for making you feel happy, rushing to your brain. However, although levels of endorphins rise in the bloodstream when you exercise, it's not clear how much actually gets into the brain. Research into this is still being carried out. The part of the brain that responds strongly to exercise is called the hippocampus. Experiments in children, adults and the elderly show that this brain structure grows as people get fitter. As the hippocampus is very important for learning and memory, this finding partly explains the memory-boosting effects of improved fitness.

C As well as slowly improving your memory, physical exercise can have a more immediate impact on the learning process itself. Researchers have shown that walking or cycling at the same time as trying to learn something new, for example foreign language vocabulary, is really helpful. So exercise while you revise. Don't push it too hard, though: extreme workouts can raise your stress levels, which, of course, can have a negative effect on your ability to remember things. Exercise can also help you to stay on task. In one study, allowing school pupils a 20-minute exercise session between lessons was found to improve their attention spans. Meanwhile, another study looked at the effects of daily after-school sports classes over a school year. The children, of course, got fitter. Less predictably, they showed greater levels of concentration in class: they became better at ignoring distractions and remembering and using what they'd learnt.

D And you may not have to get out of breath to improve your attention span. Just 10 minutes of play aimed at improving coordination skills, like bouncing two balls at the same time, has been shown to have real benefits for people's ability to concentrate. A lot of people have claimed that doing physical exercise, even just walking, makes you able to think more imaginatively. Psychologists have now found this to be the case. Walking, either outdoors or on a treadmill in a gym, can boost creative thinking. On the other hand, if you're struggling with your homework and looking for a single solution to a maths problem, then a relaxing walk isn't necessarily what you need. It seems that what you do with your body will inevitably affect your brain and how well you're able to learn new things. So get up and get active!

WRITING (1 hour 20 minutes)

Part 1

You **must** answer this question. Write your answer in **140–190** words in an appropriate style on the separate answer sheet.

---

1 In your English class you have been talking about physical appearance. Now your English teacher has asked you to write an essay.

Write your essay using **all** the notes and giving reasons for your point of view.

'We are much too worried about how people and things look.'
Do you agree?

Notes

Write about:

1. being like your friends
2. the effect of celebrities
3. .... (your own idea)

 → p. 100

Part 2

Write an answer to **one** of the questions **2–4** in this part. Write your answer in **140–190** words in an appropriate style on the separate answer sheet. Put the question number in the box at the top of the answer sheet.

---

2 You receive this email from your English friend, Sam.

> Hi
>
> I'm visiting relatives in Scotland next week. It's a ten-hour train ride! I know that you do quite a bit of long-distance travelling. What do you take with you on a long journey? And what can I do so I don't get bored?
>
> Thanks
>
> Sam

Write your **email**.

3 You see this notice in an English-language magazine for teenagers.

> **Articles wanted**
>
> **My life at the moment!**
>
> Write an article for our magazine, explaining what you like about your life at the moment. How do you think your life will change over the next couple of years, and why?
>
> The best articles will appear in our magazine next month.

Write your **article**.

4 You have seen this announcement in an international magazine for teenagers.

> **Stories wanted**
>
> We are looking for stories for our new English-language magazine for teenagers. Your story must **begin** with this sentence:
>
> *It was Tom's first deep-sea diving lesson and he felt quite nervous.*
>
> Your story must include:
>
> - a shark
> - a photograph

Write your **story**.

→ p. 102

LISTENING (approximately 40 minutes)

Part 1

Listening test audio

You will hear people talking in eight different situations.
For questions **1–8**, choose the best answer (**A**, **B** or **C**).

---

1 You hear two students discussing some research into the behaviour of fish.

How does the girl feel about the research?

A confused about how the study was conducted

B surprised by the ability the fish displayed

C amused by the subject of the experiment

2 You hear a boy telling his friend about an important football match he will play in soon.

What does he decide to do?

A recommend that another player should join the team

B request further practice sessions before the game

C ask the coach to change his position on the field

3 You hear two friends talking about a rock band.

They agree that the band members

A had become tired from working too hard.

B were likely to have arguments.

C had very different ideas about music.

4 You hear a teacher talking to his class after a discussion on space exploration.

What is he doing?

A challenging his students' point of view

B asking his students to support their argument

C praising his students for reaching agreement

5 You hear two friends talking about a riverboat trip they've been on.

What do they both think made it worthwhile?

A the information provided

B the music on board

C the views of the city

6 You hear a boy talking about working as a volunteer in a nature reserve.

What did he feel about the experience?

A surprised by how rewarding he found it

B disappointed that he couldn't choose what to do

C pleased that he could show how much he knew

7 You hear a radio news item about National Ice Cream Month in the USA.

What is one ice cream company doing to mark the event?

A designing stamps with illustrations of ice cream on them

B manufacturing a range of ice cream with fewer calories

C introducing some different varieties of ice cream

8 You hear a girl talking about a science project she did at school.

What does she say about the project?

A It helped her with other studies.

B It was interesting to take part in.

C It took too long to set up.

→ p. 110 p. 111

Part 2

You will hear a man called Ben Gardener talking about his job, making large models from plastic building blocks. For questions **9–18**, complete the sentences with a word or short phrase.

Listening test audio

Ben Gardener – model maker

Ben was an engineer in the field of **(9)** .... , before getting his current job.

Ben feels his qualification in **(10)** .... has been a great help to him in his job.

At the selection day he attended, Ben had difficulty making something that was **(11)** .... in shape.

To show his range of skills, Ben chose to make a model of a **(12)** ....

When designing a model, Ben's **(13)** .... are more helpful to him than anything else.

Ben's models are glued together to prevent them from being broken when **(14)** .... touch them.

Ben particularly enjoys working on the **(15)** .... that will accompany a moving model.

Ben recalls that he had to climb into a huge model of a **(16)** .... to make it secure.

Ben's next job will be to construct a model of a **(17)** .... from bricks.

Before making a model of a building, Ben has to visit it to get the correct **(18)** .... of the place.

→ p. 110 | p. 115

Part 3

You will hear five short extracts in which teenagers are talking about their experience of speaking in public. For questions **19–23**, choose from the list (**A–H**) what each speaker felt about the experience. Use the letters only once. There are three extra letters which you do not need to use.

Listening test audio

A discouraged by how good other people were

B proud of having done detailed research

C disappointed to have felt so nervous

D relieved not to have made any mistakes

E embarrassed at having to change the plan at the last moment

F grateful to have been given support

G annoyed that their efforts were not appreciated

H surprised that practising didn't help much

Speaker 1		**19**
Speaker 2		**20**
Speaker 3		**21**
Speaker 4		**22**
Speaker 5		**23**

→ p. 110 p. 117

Part 4

You will hear an interview with a student called Laura Benson, who is talking about her experience of studying caterpillars and other insects in a rainforest in Central America. For questions **24–30**, choose the best answer (**A**, **B** or **C**).

Listening test audio

---

24 What was the first thing that surprised Laura about the rainforest?

A how hot it was

B how noisy it was

C how colourful it was

25 Why was the task of collecting caterpillars difficult for Laura?

A The idea of handling them made her feel nervous.

B Their appearance made them hard to see.

C She was unsure where to look for them.

26 A scientist from Mexico that Laura worked with was studying

A how caterpillars digest their food.

B how caterpillars defend themselves.

C how caterpillars adapt to their environment.

27 What did Laura enjoy taking photographs of?

A different shapes that caterpillars form

B previously unknown species of caterpillar

C the process of caterpillars becoming butterflies

28 What does Laura think is the most important thing she learned about caterpillars?

A how much damage they can cause to crops

B how little is known about them

C how significant they are for other wildlife

29 How does Laura now feel about a jungle hike she went on?

A embarrassed about how she behaved at times

B sorry she was unable to repeat the experience

C proud to have overcome very challenging conditions

30 As a result of her rainforest experiences, Laura thinks that in future she is likely to

A get involved in work to protect the environment.

B continue with her education.

C do research into different species of insects.

→ p. 110 p. 119

Test 2

READING AND USE OF ENGLISH (1 hour 15 minutes)

Part 1

For questions **1–8**, read the text below and decide which answer (**A**, **B**, **C** or **D**) best fits each gap. There is an example at the beginning (**0**).

Mark your answers on the separate answer sheet.

Example:

0 **A** great **B** high **C** wide **D** strong

0	A	B	C	D
	o	●	o	o

Pigeons monitor air pollution levels in London

A team of racing pigeons flew over London recently in order to collect information on the UK capital's **(0)** .... pollution levels. The birds were each carrying a small lightweight backpack containing an air quality monitor which **(1)** .... measured levels of polluting gases as the birds flew around the city. The project wasn't **(2)** .... to be a permanent solution to air monitoring in London. It only lasted for three days, and was more concerned with raising awareness about the scale of the city's pollution problem.

People interested in finding out about the air quality in their area could send a message to the organisers **(3)** .... the internet. They then got an automated **(4)** .... , rating it on a scale of 'Fresh' to 'Extreme'.

Any attempt to improve air quality should be **(5)** .... by Londoners. And **(6)** .... residents aren't generally great fans of pigeons, this **(7)** .... flock of helpful racing pigeons may have changed some people's **(8)** .... to the birds.

1	**A** entirely	**B** intensively	**C** endlessly	**D** constantly
2	**A** intended	**B** imagined	**C** arranged	**D** advised
3	**A** down	**B** with	**C** over	**D** along
4	**A** response	**B** return	**C** reaction	**D** repeat
5	**A** greeted	**B** received	**C** welcomed	**D** awarded
6	**A** despite	**B** although	**C** however	**D** even
7	**A** certain	**B** particular	**C** exact	**D** precise
8	**A** idea	**B** opinion	**C** view	**D** attitude

→ p. 121

Part 2

For questions **9–16**, read the text below and think of the word which best fits each gap. Use only **one** word in each gap. There is an example at the beginning (**0**).

Write your answers **IN CAPITAL LETTERS on the separate answer sheet**.

Example: | **0** | T | H | E |

Ice car racing

From January to March **(0)** .... temperature in the US state of Minnesota often drops to -40°C. That's when, in **(9)** .... to show off their driving skills, some people go to the area's frozen lakes that double up as racetracks. The cars used are standard family-type cars fitted with special tyres, designed **(10)** .... ensure they don't skid on the slippery ice.

The races are organised once the ice layer **(11)** .... reached a thickness of 46 cm. A maximum of ten cars take **(12)** .... in each race. With multiple cars racing around the track at speeds of 160 kmph, you might expect collisions to **(13)** .... a regular occurrence. In fact, that is not the case. **(14)** .... there have been minor accidents, the main hazard is flying snow dust rather than other cars.

Minnesota is not the **(15)** .... state to host such events. The sport is also popular in New York and Alaska, as **(16)** .... as in the Canadian provinces and parts of Europe.

 → p. 121

Part 3

For questions **17–24**, read the text below. Use the word given in capitals at the end of some of the lines to form a word that fits in the gap **in the same line**. There is an example at the beginning (**0**).

Write your answers **IN CAPITAL LETTERS on the separate answer sheet.**

Example:	**0**	E	X	C	I	T	E	D

Wild camping

I really enjoy camping with my dad, so I was very	
(0) .... when he suggested going wild camping – that's	**EXCITE**
camping in the middle of nowhere rather than at a campsite. This	
is not ideal for **(17)** .... campers, who might lack the	**EXPERIENCE**
necessary **(18)** .... skills. And you can't just camp	**SURVIVE**
anywhere – it may be necessary to ask for **(19)** .... But	**PERMIT**
my dad and I have been on many camping trips, and love the feeling	
of **(20)** .... it gives us. We were just being a bit more	**INDEPENDENT**
(21) .... this time.	**ADVENTURE**
One downside on a trip like this can be the unpredictable British	
weather, but we'd taken that into **(22)** .... and	**CONSIDER**
had plenty of warm clothes. Food's important too, of course.	
(23) .... , Dad and I aren't good cooks and I didn't really	**FORTUNATE**
enjoy our meals.	
However, nothing else I've done has given me the same sense	
of freedom as wild camping. Without a doubt it was the most	
(24) .... trip I've ever been on.	**MEMORY**

→ p. 121

Part 4

For questions **25–30**, complete the second sentence so that it has a similar meaning to the first sentence, using the word given. **Do not change the word given.** You must use between **two** and **five** words, including the word given. Here is an example (**0**).

Example:

0 Prizes are given out when the school year finishes.

PLACE

Prize-giving .... end of the school year.

The gap can be filled by the words 'takes place at the', so you write:

Example:	**0**	*TAKES PLACE AT THE*

Write **only** the missing words **IN CAPITAL LETTERS on the separate answer sheet.**

---

25 'You should watch the new documentary on penguins,' Nola told me.

ADVISED

Nola .... the new documentary on penguins.

26 The result was so surprising that it was impossible for anyone to predict.

SUCH

No one could ever .... surprising result.

27 My grandmother thinks that using mobile phones in restaurants is rude.

USE

My grandmother thinks that it .... mobile phones in restaurants.

28 'You can't cycle on the road without a helmet,' said Laura.

UNLESS

'You can't cycle on the road ………………………………………………………on a helmet,' said Laura.

29 'I don't think there's any milk left,' said Mum.

RUN

'We seem …………………………………………………… milk,' said Mum.

30 'I didn't see Dan at volleyball practice yesterday,' said Chris.

SIGN

'There …………………………………………………… Dan at volleyball practice yesterday,' said Chris.

→ p. 121

Part 5

You are going to read a magazine article about designing rollercoasters for amusement parks. For questions **31–36**, choose the answer (**A**, **B**, **C** or **D**) which you think fits best according to the text.

Mark your answers on the separate answer sheet.

Rollercoasters

Journalist Kashmira Gander found out about how rollercoasters are designed.

Imagine you're on a rollercoaster in an amusement park. Palms clammy with fear, nails digging into the harness, you come to a grinding halt and inhale sharply before the carriage creeps slowly upwards. A pause. Then a sharp drop and your stomach is suspended in the air. Teeth gritted, you hurtle quickly forwards, sharply left, then upside down. Your senses a blur, you let out a roar of fear that comes from the pit of your gut. But you only have yourself to blame: after all, like hundreds of millions of others each year, you were happy to pay the price of getting into a theme park.

What's somewhat mystifying to me is that amusement parks, with their hair-raising rides aimed at pulling in crowds, are a huge industry. To deliver the thrills and ultimate-escape-from-reality that guests seek, behind the scenes there are huge teams of highly inventive – and arguably a little cruel – structural, mechanical, industrial and electrical engineers, as well as designers and marketing experts.

'Rollercoaster designer' sounds like the career aspiration of a primary school child when asked what they want to be when they grow up. In reality, it's a big challenge: not just creating the perfect balance of pleasure and fear while ensuring that passengers are not in any danger, but also introducing enough novelty to keep visitors wanting more.

While the layperson may imagine that rollercoasters have become ever more intense, in fact, most of the techniques used today – including the wheel that allows rides to go upside-down – were invented by the USA designer John Miller in the early 20th century.

I spoke to three experts on rollercoasters. 'The skill,' said Professor Brendan Walker, a 'thrill engineer' with a background in aeronautics, 'is in compiling the pieces.' And what that means, said Dr John Roberts, a fellow of the Royal Academy of Engineering, is 'swapping very rapidly between plus and minus, so people get the sense of being sort of thrown around but kept safe. It's a very fine line between people feeling the ride is thrilling and that feeling they've been bumped around.'

In the search for a superlative ride, the teams behind rollercoasters must piece together a strong narrative, be it a space adventure or a high-paced chase in the jungle, that works with any innovations – the tallest ride, the most twists, the steepest drops – to create a seamless experience. However, said Professor Walker, in the end, as in many creative industries, gut instincts, years of experience and trial-and-error are what work. 'It helps to be a bit of a thrill-nut if you are designing rollercoasters, in order to understand exactly what passengers are looking for, and to test your rides before they're opened to the public,' agreed Jeff Hornick, a senior director of theme park development.

Surely though, I asked them, as technology has transformed industry after industry, rollercoaster designers will also have to embrace the latest advances, such as virtual reality? Walker said we shouldn't hold our breath. 'Virtual reality can add a veneer, but only in the way that an old fashioned rollercoaster was fantastically painted,' he said. 'New technology comes along all the time, and the parks are very quick to embrace it because it is exciting and can add to ride experience. But underpinning that is the physical coaster experience, and I think that will remain king for many years to come.'

31 What does the writer say in the first paragraph about people who ride on rollercoasters?

A They spend too much money trying to find excitement.
B They can't complain when they feel terrified.
C They often don't realise how frightening the experience will be.
D They should try to control their emotions more effectively.

32 What do we learn in the second paragraph about the writer's attitude towards rollercoasters?

A She is concerned that they may have a negative effect on passengers.
B She believes they promise more excitement than they can deliver.
C She regrets that people feel the need to spend their leisure time in this way.
D She finds it hard to understand why so much effort is put into creating them.

33 What is suggested about rollercoaster designers in the third paragraph?

A They have had the courage to follow their dreams.
B They should try harder to please theme park visitors.
C They deserve credit for doing a demanding job effectively.
D They are not the kind of people who can be taken seriously.

34 What is emphasised by 'it's a very fine line' in lines 46 and 47?

A how very unpredictable people are
B the speed at which so many rides can go
C the possible risks involved in going on a ride
D how difficult it is to get a ride exactly right

35 What does 'that' refer to in line 53?

A a superlative ride
B a strong narrative
C a space adventure
D a high-paced chase

36 What does Walker suggest about new technology in the rollercoaster industry?

A Designers are reluctant to use it.
B It has proved problematic in the past.
C It has a limited role to play.
D Passengers rarely notice its impact.

→ p. 121

Part 6

You are going to read a magazine article about communication between trees. Six sentences have been removed from the article. Choose from the sentences **A–G** the one which fits each gap (**37–42**). There is one extra sentence which you do not need to use.

Mark your answers on the separate answer sheet.

How trees communicate

Can trees communicate with each other? Surprisingly, the answer seems to be that they can. Forest ecologist Dr Suzanne Simard, from the University of British Columbia in Canada, has been studying tiny living organisms, or fungi, which form underground communication networks between trees in North American forests. Big old trees, nicknamed 'mother trees', are central to this network, playing a key role in supporting smaller trees in the forest – in particular, their own offspring.

Simard explains that if you're a mother, you put your children first and tend to give them special treatment. **37** In situations where they would normally compete with other trees, they adjust their behaviour to make room for their own family members. They communicate their presence through their fungal networks, so when a very young tree tries to establish itself on the forest floor, it can just link into the mother tree's root systems and so join the fungal network, taking advantage of its considerable resources.

What is more, these networks don't just operate between related trees. They may also form between different species in the same community. For example, Simard also traced the amounts of carbon, nitrogen and water moving between a Douglas fir and a paper birch tree, both native to the forests of British Columbia. In one experiment a tree was artificially prevented from getting the light it needed to grow healthily. **38** The nutrients it needed flowed into the tree from others, through the networks between them.

In another study, Simard showed that within a 30 by 30 metre wooded area, an estimated 250 to 300 different trees were connected by fungal networks. This is of huge benefit to the trees and these networks allow a wider variety of tree types to survive in one area. **39** This diversity creates a basis for a forest that's resilient to disease, climate change and pests such as insects.

Other research has suggested that trees use fungal networks to warn their neighbours about impending attacks from pests. According to Simard, when trees are attacked, they increase their own protection against the invaders by producing a substance which helps them to defend themselves. **40** When these messages are detected, the other trees upgrade their protection systems by producing chemicals of their own.

41 Western Australia, for example, is dominated by healthy trees that don't rely on them, possibly due to the fact that the soil there is richer in nutrients. However, Australian Eucalyptus forests do have networks, although no research has yet been done into what their function might be.

Simard believes her findings have implications for forestry practices which involve the cutting down of old trees. 'We need to leave these trees standing so that they are able to send their messages into the soil to surrounding plants.' Forests are frequently damaged by fire, she says. **42** And it may be that protecting old trees will not only contribute to the restoration of these wooded areas, but may also prevent non-native species from invading them.

A Each species has its own strengths and weaknesses.

B These can travel between trees in as little as six hours.

C As they do this, chemical signals pass through their networks to nearby trees.

D In response, the surrounding trees began to share resources rather than compete for them.

E Whether fungal networks are used may depend on the local ecosystem.

F Conserving their networks could help them recover after such an event.

G Research suggests that trees do the same thing.

→ p. 121

Part 7

You are going to read a magazine article in which four different people talk about their favourite science fiction books. For questions **43–52**, choose from the people (**A–D**). The people may be chosen more than once.

Mark your answers on the separate answer sheet.

Which person

immediately felt familiar with the subject matter of the book?	**43**	
says that the book has influenced how they judge other science fiction novels?	**44**	
mentions that their interest in sci-fi was maintained by this book?	**45**	
appreciated the fact that the writer gives readers the opportunity to use their imagination?	**46**	
found elements in the book of a type of story they disliked?	**47**	
initially struggled to understand what was happening in the novel?	**48**	
doubts whether many writers would be capable of producing something similar?	**49**	
enjoyed the opportunity to see things from a completely different point of view?	**50**	
was given the book because of their love of a particular location?	**51**	
finds the characters in the book are familiar, despite their origins?	**52**	

 → p. 121

Favourite science fiction books

A Tom

I have to admit it took me a while to finish this novel. The story involves a group of friends with special powers who are now being called on to help save the world. Every time I stumbled across someone that felt like a superhero from comics, I'd put it down again in disgust, as their plots had always felt so predictable to me. When I finally got down to giving the book my full attention, I realised what I'd been missing. What the author does is to use the story to crack open a much deeper issue – moral, philosophical, whatever. And every detail counts, as he really stretches the boundaries of storytelling in ways most authors wouldn't even attempt, let alone be able to pull off. Some readers will disagree, I know, but I now compare any sci-fi book I read with this one – and most of them fall short.

B James

In my opinion, you can't write science fiction well if you haven't read any – but then neither can you write it if you haven't read anything else. Many authors just use jargon which makes their work meaningful only to a limited group of fans. When I first started reading this novel by an author who's better known for literary fiction, I found the plot rather confusing, but soon discovered that the fantasy world she'd created was brought dramatically alive by her skill. I was transported to the past and the future by her unusual imagery, which left out just enough detail to allow me to fill in the gaps and form my own idea of her world. In this story, the writer gets inside the mind of a dog – a non-human brain, and an alien mentality. We're invited to picture the dog's timeless world, and experience everyday life through eyes other than our own. That to me is the essence of true sci-fi.

C Anna

One of my favourite haunts has always been the vast heated greenhouse in the botanical garden in my city. And the more spiked and monster-like the plants that are growing there, the more fascinating I find them. So when I mentioned this to my mum, she spotted an opportunity to interest me in literature, and presented me with *Plant Monsters*. I read it in one sitting, excited by an instant sense of recognition. After all, I knew these plants already. What appealed, I think, was the writer's love of addressing the great 'What if...?' questions: what if monster plants such as these broke loose and started to take over the planet? Enter the hero Jamie King, tasked with saving the world. Yet it's the plants that root themselves most firmly in the reader's memory. The writer describes them in great detail botanically, but in my mind's eye they were the ones growing in a greenhouse – right in the heart of my city.

D Sarah

It wasn't easy to pick just one book as my favourite by this writer. She's written so many, all of which I've read, and all of them are weird but somehow true. Fantasy and sci-fi get mixed up with domestic family tales so that awkward teenagers are having to cope with mythological creatures and superhuman powers. I loved sci-fi even before I read these books, but might have outgrown it had it not been for *Universe* and its characters. The book's about other worlds, which I loved, but the people in it are very much of this one. They're eccentric, lonely, funny, sometimes selfish, but always characters I can identify with. I find it really interesting to discover how they make their way through the situations they find themselves in. And her interesting insights into why children can have problems with other family members during their teenage years have been a very helpful guide to me.

WRITING (1 hour 20 minutes)

Part 1

You **must** answer this question. Write your answer in **140–190** words in an appropriate style on the separate answer sheet.

---

1 In your English class you have been talking about school life. Now your English teacher has asked you to write an essay.

Write your essay using **all** the notes and giving reasons for your point of view.

Do you think that students should help to make decisions about what happens at school?

Notes

Write about:

1. the subjects children study

2. school rules

3. .... (your own idea)

 → p. 103

Part 2

Write an answer to **one** of the questions **2–4** in this part. Write your answer in **140–190** words in an appropriate style on the separate answer sheet. Put the question number in the box at the top of the answer sheet.

---

2 You see this notice in an English-language magazine.

> **Articles wanted**
>
> **Someone famous**
>
> If you could meet a famous person, who would you choose? In your article explain why you would like to meet this person. What kinds of things would you like to talk about?
>
> The best articles will be published in our magazine.

Write your **article**.

3 You see this advert on a website about sports.

> Reviews wanted
>
> **Sports shop**
>
> We're looking for reviews of shops which sell sportswear and sports equipment.
>
> Write a review of a sports shop which you use.
>
> In your review you should:
>
> - describe the shop and what it sells
> - explain what you especially like about it
> - say why you'd recommend the shop to other young people.

Write your **review**.

4 You receive this email from your English friend, Mel.

> Hi
>
> There's a problem which I definitely need some help with. I've got a friend, Chris, who's always borrowing things from me (and other people), but who doesn't return them.
>
> Thanks for your help.
>
> Mel

Write your **email**.

→ p. 104

LISTENING (approximately 40 minutes)

Listening test audio

Part 1

You will hear people talking in eight different situations.
For questions **1–8**, choose the best answer (**A**, **B** or **C**).

---

1 You hear a girl telling a friend about a family trip she went on to a climbing centre.

What does she feel about the trip now?

A She regrets not taking part in more activities.

B She wishes it hadn't become so competitive.

C She realises they should have researched it better.

2 You hear a teacher talking to her class about a visit to a science exhibition.

What does she recommend they do during the visit?

A refer to material they'll be taking with them

B prepare to do homework based on their observations

C select demonstrations related to their course

3 You hear two students discussing a film they saw on TV.

What do the students agree about?

A The actors suited the roles they played.

B The plot had some unexpected developments.

C The director made some unusual choices.

4 You hear a woman talking about her work as a fashion designer.

What is she doing?

A describing how her attitude to clothes changed when she was younger

B criticising people whose taste in clothes is different from hers

C explaining how her ideas about clothes developed

5 You hear a student talking about a project he has done on bees.

What is unusual about the bees he is describing?

A The way they find food.

B The conditions in which they survive.

C The fact they build their nests underground.

6 You hear a girl talking about giving up social media for two weeks.

What does she say about her experience?

A It had some rather unexpected results.

B It turned out to be impossible for her to do.

C It was hard to deal with other people's reactions.

7 You hear a teacher telling his students about some research into learning and memory.

What was the result of the research?

A Music can negatively affect the ability to remember words and images.

B Associating words with images can aid memory.

C Images aren't as easy to recall as words.

8 You hear a girl talking about the choir she sings in.

What did the choir appreciate about a recent event?

A singing inside a historic building

B getting singing lessons from an expert

C performing with professional singers

→ p. 122 p. 123

Part 2

You will hear a girl called Kelly talking about an activity called potholing, which involves exploring underground caves. For questions **9–18**, complete the sentences with a word or short phrase.

Listening test audio

Potholing

Kelly's uncle started exploring caves because he is interested in

(9) ....

Kelly's first experience of potholing was to a local cave called

(10) ....

Kelly was very pleased to see **(11)** .... inside the first cave she explored.

Kelly had a problem with her **(12)** .... the first time she went into a cave.

In her first cave, Kelly noticed some rocks that reminded her of a

(13) ....

On her first expedition, Kelly complained that her

(14) .... was painful.

Kelly says that professional people who explore caves particularly worry about

(15) ....

Kelly says that a **(16)** .... is the most important piece of equipment to take underground.

On Kelly's second trip, her biggest challenge was managing to get through a

(17) ....

Kelly's most memorable experience was seeing some

(18) .... lighting up a cave she was exploring.

 → p. 122 p. 127

Part 3

You will hear five short extracts in which teenagers are talking about a journey they recently went on. For questions **19–23**, choose from the list **(A–H)** what each speaker says about the experience. Use the letters only once. There are three extra letters which you do not need to use.

Listening test audio

A It was more comfortable than I thought it would be.

B Meeting someone took my mind off my problems.

C A careless mistake almost meant that the trip didn't go ahead.

D I was glad I ignored some advice I was given.

E There was an unexpected long-term consequence.

F I had the opportunity to use a new skill.

G It was satisfying to help a travelling companion.

H I regretted leaving something at home.

Speaker 1		**19**
Speaker 2		**20**
Speaker 3		**21**
Speaker 4		**22**
Speaker 5		**23**

→ p. 122 p. 129

Part 4

You will hear an interview with a school student from Scotland, called Jake Dawson, who is talking about cycling in the snow in a town in Finland. For questions **24–30**, choose the best answer (**A**, **B** or **C**).

Listening test audio

24 What similarity did Jake notice between his hometown and the town in Finland?

A the attractiveness of the architecture

B the quality of the light in winter

C the liveliness of the streets

25 The weather in Finland made Jake realise that in Scotland

A he hadn't gone out in winter as much as he should have done.

B he had spent too much time inside a car in winter.

C he hadn't appreciated how beautiful winter could be.

26 Jake says people in Scotland don't cycle much in the snow because

A they think it's too cold.

B they don't have the right equipment.

C the conditions on the roads are too dangerous.

27 What did Jake like about cycling in the snow in the Finnish town?

A Underpasses enabled cyclists to avoid busy junctions.

B Motorists showed respect to cyclists.

C Cycle paths were kept clear of snow.

28 What does Jake say about his experience of cycling across a frozen river?

A He was keen to take advantage of a unique opportunity.

B He lost his nerve before reaching the other side.

C He felt relieved to be doing it with his cousin.

29 What happened to Jake on one occasion while cycling in the snow?

A He missed a road sign and lost his way.

B He made a mistake and hit another cyclist.

C He became overconfident and fell off his bike.

30 Jake decided that when he got back to Scotland, he would

A buy himself a better quality bike.

B use the cycling techniques he'd learned.

C persuade his friends to take up cycling.

→ p. 122 p. 131

Test 3

READING AND USE OF ENGLISH (1 hour 15 minutes)

Part 1

For questions **1–8**, read the text below and decide which answer (**A**, **B**, **C** or **D**) best fits each gap. There is an example at the beginning (**0**).

Mark your answers on the separate answer sheet.

Example:

0 **A** thought **B** known **C** seen **D** noticed

0	A	B	C	D
	o	●	o	o

The glass bridge

There are many bridges in the world, but some are **(0)** .... for more than just connecting one place to another. In China, for example, the Zhangjiajie Bridge has already **(1)** .... records for being the highest and longest in the world.

The bridge crosses a deep valley, **(2)** .... two mountain cliffs, with a **(3)** .... of 300 metres below. It is made almost **(4)** .... of glass and can carry up to 800 people at a time. They can either walk across it, or the more adventurous can bungee-jump from it. Questions have been **(5)** .... about whether the transparent glass floor is safe, but it has been assessed, and **(6)** .... have been given that the glass just won't break. In fact a media event was organised, where people were invited to try to **(7)** .... the bridge's glass panels with huge hammers. They were unable to.

Everyone who has tried crossing the Zhangjiajie bridge says it's an experience not to be **(8)** .... However, tourists do have to book tickets in advance.

1	**A**	made	**B**	put	**C**	set	**D**	taken
2	**A**	linking	**B**	uniting	**C**	combining	**D**	attaching
3	**A**	descent	**B**	dip	**C**	decline	**D**	drop
4	**A**	absolutely	**B**	entirely	**C**	specifically	**D**	particularly
5	**A**	enquired	**B**	raised	**C**	requested	**D**	demanded
6	**A**	assurances	**B**	reports	**C**	statements	**D**	announcements
7	**A**	harm	**B**	slam	**C**	smash	**D**	crash
8	**A**	lost	**B**	missed	**C**	passed	**D**	left

→ p. 133

Part 2

For questions **9–16**, read the text below and think of the word which best fits each gap. Use only **one** word in each gap. There is an example at the beginning (**0**).

Write your answers **IN CAPITAL LETTERS on the separate answer sheet.**

Example: | 0 | *T H E* |

'Read and Ride'

Schools across **(0)** .... world are always thinking of new ways to keep students active and alert. A school in the USA has recently installed exercise bikes in one classroom and students ride these while reading their books. A staff member at the school, **(9)** .... enjoys using an exercise bike at the gym and reading at the same time, came **(10)** .... with the idea for **(11)** .... he calls the 'Read and Ride' program. Believing this would be a fun way to persuade students to become more active, he placed one in his classroom and encouraged them to use **(12)** .... during independent reading sessions.

The exercise bike was **(13)** .... a success that he introduced the Read and Ride program to the entire school. Now the school has a special room full of bikes that **(14)** .... regularly used by students. Besides **(15)** .... reading more fun, the program also helps students to exercise at a comfortable pace without experiencing the pressure that comes **(16)** .... competitive sports.

 → p. 133

Part 3

For questions **17–24**, read the text below. Use the word given in capitals at the end of some of the lines to form a word that fits in the gap **in the same line**. There is an example at the beginning (**0**).

Write your answers **IN CAPITAL LETTERS on the separate answer sheet.**

Example: | 0 | N E E D L E S S |

The Real Junk Food Project

In many countries there's a lot of **(0)** .... food waste. **NEED**
Some people think this is **(17)** .... and want to **ACCEPT**
persuade supermarkets to reduce the amount of food they
throw away. One reason for the problem is that some customers
are very **(18)** .... , especially when it comes to the **DEMAND**
(19) .... of the food they buy. **APPEAR**

(20) .... , fruit and vegetables that are in any way **CONSEQUENCE**
(21) .... , perhaps because they're a strange shape, are **PERFECT**
considered unsuitable for sale.

The Real Junk Food Project was started in the UK by a chef, Adam
Smith. He opened a café where the entire menu was produced
from ingredients that would have been wasted. There were no fixed
prices, customers were simply asked to pay what they felt the food
was worth. The project has provided the **(22)** .... behind **INSPIRE**
similar cafés around the world. Of course, if supermarkets are
(23) .... persuaded to stop wasting food these cafés **SUCCESS**
won't survive, but that's been Adam's **(24)** .... from the **INTEND**
start!

→ p. 133

Part 4

For questions **25–30**, complete the second sentence so that it has a similar meaning to the first sentence, using the word given. **Do not change the word given.** You must use between **two** and **five** words, including the word given. Here is an example (**0**).

Example:

0 Prizes are given out when the school year finishes.

PLACE

Prize-giving .... end of the school year.

The gap can be filled by the words 'takes place at the', so you write:

Example:	**0**	*TAKES PLACE AT THE*

Write **only** the missing words **IN CAPITAL LETTERS on the separate answer sheet.**

---

25 The students couldn't believe they'd lost the football match.

IMPOSSIBLE

The students found .... believe they'd lost the football match.

26 I'm sure it was Lucas who ate the last biscuit.

MUST

Lucas .... the last biscuit.

27 The students are watching a film about climate change.

BEING

A film about climate change .... to the students.

28 Don't take my word for it, check with the teacher.

BELIEVE

You don't .... say, check with the teacher.

29 This is the best pizza restaurant in the area, in my opinion.

CONCERNED

As .... , this is the best pizza restaurant in the area.

30 More people have joined the school tennis club this year.

INCREASE

There .... in the number of people joining the school tennis club this year.

→ p. 133

Part 5

You are going to read an extract from an interview with a young choreographer, someone who creates and arranges new dances. For questions **31–36**, choose the answer (**A**, **B**, **C** or **D**) which you think fits best according to the text.

Mark your answers on the separate answer sheet.

Interview with a young choreographer

Martin Fields talks to Miranda Ellington about her life and work.

At 25, Miranda Ellington has already achieved a great deal as a choreographer, creating works for a long list of theatres and dance companies. On top of that, she still dances from time to time. 'Being a dancer again reminds me of what it feels like to be in the studio taking orders from demanding choreographers, and how tense and frustrating that can be. Choreographers can lose sight of what it's like to be rehearsing all day long,' she tells me.

As a choreographer, she is essentially in a teaching role and enjoys working with young students. 'A dancer who's just starting out is often receptive to exploring new ideas. In some ways, working with students is easier than with professionals because they're open to taking risks. They're hungry for success, but they don't yet have a clear sense of their strengths and weaknesses. The incomplete picture they have of their skills ensures they take on board even quite harsh criticism. They might still challenge what I say sometimes, though when they do I welcome their honest feedback.'

When Miranda starts working with a new group, the music dictates what she does. 'There may be a piece of music I'm not keen on, but I still make sure I come up with the best possible dance routine to accompany it. If dancers aren't responding well to a particular composer's music, that can be frustrating, but I'm still required to find solutions. That won't involve going back to the drawing board and selecting a new piece, though. Ideally, I'd like to be more experimental and be given the option of switching to different pieces – it'd certainly help to lift the mood when things get tough in rehearsals. Unfortunately, these days I'm always working on big productions – the musical score has already been written by the composer and it isn't negotiable.'

The conversation turns to the recent documentary on professional ballet dancers and choreographers. 'This one attempts to give viewers an accurate portrayal of life inside a dance company. There was one scene where a young dancer is getting endless corrections and I smiled in recognition when I saw it. She knows she's not getting it right but just can't make her body do what's required. It's painful to watch but not at all manufactured for the cameras. The amount of work and dedication involved in ballet is underestimated by the public.'

I'm curious to know what makes a great production. 'It's when everything the company has invested in – the music, the costumes, the lighting, and the dancers – all come together. Aiming high is appreciated by audiences and will allow you to get away with a few wrong artistic decisions or choices. I've even been involved in productions where the dance steps are great but something about the costumes or props completely distracts. And that's just disappointing.'

Miranda has done such a range of work I wonder how she sees herself: is she a modern dance choreographer or a ballet specialist? 'People seem to want to put a label on you and I can't quite understand that. And there's the modern tendency to encourage the development of expertise in a narrow area, too. I tend not to go along with that, though the time may come when I'm happy to have a reputation largely for doing one thing. For now, I just want to widen my horizons.'

31 Miranda says that she dances occasionally so that she

A can convince other choreographers to be more understanding.
B can find ways to reduce the workload for everyone involved.
C responds appropriately to any guidance she is given.
D remains aware of the pressures dancers face.

32 What does Miranda say about the students she works with?

A Their lack of confidence means they rarely question instructions.
B Their inexperience makes them willing to listen.
C Their determination to succeed can sometimes cause misunderstandings.
D Their enthusiasm sometimes means they do not see their faults.

33 When discussing the music she works with, Miranda points out that

A she is unable to ask for changes to be made.
B she often varies it to create a happy atmosphere.
C she sometimes gets annoyed with the attitude of the composer.
D she produces a better dance routine if she appreciates the music.

34 What does Miranda feel about the scene in the TV programme she mentions?

A She is unhappy about the way the dancer was treated.
B She is worried that it exaggerates how hard dancing can be.
C She is pleased that it reveals the truth about being a dancer.
D She is proud of the dancer's attempts to improve herself.

35 Miranda says that productions she's worked on can sometimes

A combine too many elements in one performance.
B be spoilt by a problem outside her control.
C fail to win people's complete approval.
D lack the resources that she expects.

36 In the final paragraph Miranda says that she

A resists attempts to define her in a particular way.
B feels that others may have the wrong opinion of her.
C is confused by the number of career options available to her.
D doubts that specialising will benefit her in the long term.

→ p. 133

Part 6

You are going to read a newspaper article about a competition between a human and a machine. Six sentences have been removed from the article. Choose from the sentences **A–G** the one which fits each gap (**37–42**). There is one extra sentence which you do not need to use.

Mark your answers on the separate answer sheet.

Machine defeats man in complex board game

Recently, millions of people watched a man play a computer in a game called 'Go', one of the oldest board games in the world. The game involves two players placing black and white counters on a board, and gaining ground by 'capturing' their opponent's counters. It is thought to be the most complex game ever devised. A human-looking robot called AlphaGo, which was trained by a company called Deep Mind, played five games against Korean Lee Sodol, one of the world's leading players. Surprisingly, the computer won the opening game with ease.

A fellow professional player of the game, Myung-wan Kim, was interviewed soon after the result was announced. He admitted that, although he had expected that the computer would perhaps manage to win a game at some point in the tournament, he never imagined that it was going to be the very first one. **37** ____ However, it got considerably worse, as he went on to lose the next two games.

The computer revealed its calculating nature towards the end of one of the games, when it appeared to have made a mistake that allowed Lee to capture several of AlphaGo's counters. **38** ____ AlphaGo had thought ahead and made a clever tactical move. This proved it was capable of doing whatever would maximise its chances of ultimately winning. At this stage, Lee felt embarrassed about the fact that he was now losing 3-0 and stressed it was his personal defeat and not an indication that a computer like AlphaGo would always win against a human.

Lee started to fight back in the middle of the fourth game by making some astonishing moves of his own, and spectators believed he might finally get his revenge. One of Lee's old rivals, who was in the audience, praised him for the quality of his performance. Meanwhile, the assembled journalists began to take notice, as AlphaGo seemed to be struggling. **39** ____ This led some to speculate that the software was seriously malfunctioning.

Lee was now minutes away from his first victory over AlphaGo, and was calm and fully focused at this crucial moment. **40** ____ Then a message appeared on AlphaGo's screen confirming that it had conceded defeat for the first time.

41 ____ Instead, his focus was on the board and on the game he'd just won. In Go, it's customary to review the match with your opponent and to share your thoughts. Such a dialogue was not possible because across from Lee sat only the computer programmer, who was totally unable to explain the mistakes that AlphaGo had made on this occasion.

Despite this setback for AlphaGo, the overall result was still a 3-1 win for the machine. It was a significant moment in the development of artificial intelligence. **42** ____ This time, however, AlphaGo had learnt moves as a result of practical experience and had worked out the complex rules for itself – a very impressive achievement, as everyone acknowledged.

A It was starting to make increasingly erratic and strange moves, which nobody could explain.

B Although it is quite advanced, it is only by trial and error that the machine can learn in this way.

C But if Lee was quietly congratulating himself for this victory, it was barely noticeable.

D Lee felt much the same, expressing disbelief that a mere machine could play the game so skilfully.

E In past experiments, computers had been programmed with information about the game before they faced their first human opponent.

F Meanwhile, the computer's programmer, who was responsible for moving counters on the board in response to instructions from the little machine, looked tense and worried.

G Lee thought this could be a turning point, but that was not the case.

→ p. 133

Part 7

You are going to read an article about young people's experiences of learning to surf. For questions **43–52**, choose from the people (**A–D**). The people may be chosen more than once.

Mark your answers on the separate answer sheet.

Which person

admits to being in need of praise from other people?	**43**	
says that despite having some ability they didn't wish to continue?	**44**	
describes an anxiety that held them back for some time?	**45**	
mentions that a previous experience could have discouraged them from trying again?	**46**	
says that other distractions prevented them from trying surfing earlier?	**47**	
describes how someone else's enthusiasm made a big difference?	**48**	
says they appreciated learning in a methodical way?	**49**	
explains how surfing failed to have the emotional impact that others had predicted?	**50**	
mentions how the absence of spectators on the day proved helpful?	**51**	
expresses appreciation of people's tolerance?	**52**	

 → p. 133

Young surfers

A Jessica Lee

I've always had an emotional attachment to the sea which I can't quite explain. I've watched it for years, appreciating its beauty and power. But I'd never actually dared to go in. I could swim, yet something about the sea made me nervous. I knew I needed to overcome this if I wanted to fulfil my ambition of surfing. One year I finally went for it when I was on holiday. The beach was almost deserted, which was ideal as I was feeling incredibly self-conscious. The coach was so positive about everything and that really filled me with confidence. But I was so focused on remembering what to do, that by the time I finally got into the water I was no longer feeling nervous. It took a few attempts, but then suddenly I was on my feet, gliding along, so thrilled that I'd actually caught my first wave. To my astonishment, for the first time ever, I had a genuine passion for something and this took up all my spare time and completely changed my outlook on things.

B Robert Morgan

My first attempt at surfing had consisted of two miserable hours on my own getting battered by the waves, while trying to cling onto my board. This should have put me off but somehow it didn't. I decided to have another go and booked some lessons this time. The first lesson wasn't too promising, actually, because there was a whole set of warm-up exercises to do, which irritated me, but the instructor explained that without them there was a real chance of cramp and getting into difficulty in the water. Then he talked us through the basics – catching waves and controlling the board while lying on it – then sent us out into the water. When we'd mastered all that, we returned to the beach to learn the next skill. This progressive tuition was great for building confidence – attempting too much in one go would have been overwhelming. Before long, I'd got to grips with catching waves, although standing on the board out at sea proved to be rather tricky. In fact, after that initial session, I was totally exhausted and even had trouble standing up on dry land!

C Chloe Emery

The welcome from all the staff couldn't have been warmer. It would have been easy for them to look down on clueless beginners like myself. To my relief, they seemed genuinely delighted when someone finally made a breakthrough and could actually do the basics. I was very aware that I was barely keeping up with my classmates, who got the hang of the technical side surprisingly quickly. What I also found difficult was that the board was so much heavier than I'd expected and this held me back for a while. I can't really remember the first time I rode a bicycle without stabilisers, but I do remember feeling proud the first time I managed to balance independently and looked round at my father for a nod of encouragement. When I mastered the considerably more difficult skills required for surfing, I had a similar feeling. I almost felt like shouting out, 'Look, I'm doing it!' The wish to gain approval, I'm embarrassed to say, was overwhelming.

D Leo McIntyre

I'd always had glamorous images of surfing in my mind but I found that this romantic picture wasn't very accurate. Perhaps I didn't want to burst the bubble and learn how tough it was. I'd lived near the coast for a long time but couldn't tear myself away from the volleyball court long enough to take up any other sports. I loved the ocean and swam daily but somehow surfing just seemed as if it should be for super-fit, trendy people who had great balance and no fear. When I managed to surf my first wave, I was too astonished to enjoy the moment. Feelings of exhilaration and freedom are supposed to hit you – at least, that was what all my surfing friends had repeatedly told me. I didn't seem to be following the script because I felt strangely uninvolved in the experience, so this wasn't something I was going to take any further – apparently I actually showed promise but that didn't change anything.

WRITING (1 hour 20 minutes)

Part 1

You **must** answer this question. Write your answer in **140–190** words in an appropriate style on the separate answer sheet.

---

1 In your English class you have been talking about doing things on your own and with other people. Now your English teacher has asked you to write an essay.

Write your essay using **all** the notes and giving reasons for your point of view.

Some people think that it's better to do certain things alone. Do you agree?

Notes

Write about:

1. going shopping
2. studying
3. .... (your own idea)

→ p. 105

Part 2

Write an answer to **one** of the questions **2–4** in this part. Write your answer in **140–190** words in an appropriate style on the separate answer sheet. Put the question number in the box at the top of the answer sheet.

---

2 You see this notice on a film website for teenagers.

> **Reviews wanted**
>
> **Animal films**
>
> We're looking for reviews of films which have animals in them. The animals can be real or they can be cartoon characters. Explain what the film is about. Say what you think of the film and whether you'd recommend it to other young people.

Write your **review**.

3 You receive this email from your English friend, Kit.

> Hi
>
> It's my parents' wedding anniversary next month and my brother and I want to organise something really nice to celebrate it. But we want to keep it a secret from them before the day itself. What could we do to celebrate? And how can we keep it a secret?
>
> Thanks
>
> Kit

Write your **email**.

4 You have seen this announcement in an international magazine for teenagers.

> **Stories wanted**
>
> We are looking for stories for our new English-language magazine for teenagers. Your story must **begin** with this sentence:
>
> *When Jake looked over the edge he could see a frightened dog on the cliffs below.*
>
> Your story must include:
>
> - a rescue
> - a reward

Write your **story**.

→ p. 106

LISTENING (approximately 40 minutes)

Listening test audio

Part 1

You will hear people talking in eight different situations.
For questions **1–8**, choose the best answer (**A**, **B** or **C**).

---

1 You hear a girl talking about making online videos.

What does she say about her experience of making online videos?

A She tried not to worry about what other people thought.

B She believes that using good quality equipment is essential.

C She was successful because she kept experimenting.

2 You hear a girl talking about some photos her dad has taken.

She suggests her dad put the set of photos together in order to

A assess the development of his skills.

B keep a record of important memories.

C provide him with work to display in public.

3 You hear a young man talking about being an inventor.

How does he get ideas for new inventions?

A They are the result of observing daily life carefully.

B They come to him because he has a natural talent.

C They are related to things he has researched online.

4 You hear a teacher giving a talk to her class about bats.

What is the teacher doing during the talk?

A comparing the ways in which bats communicate

B explaining the diets that various species of bats require

C highlighting the methods bats use in order to survive

5 You hear a boy talking about going to take part in an archaeology project in Italy.

Why did he decide to join the project?

A to find out whether the subject would suit him as a career

B to establish whether his family has historical links with the area

C to contribute to what could be an exciting discovery

6 You hear a guide at a science museum talking about a new virtual reality device that visitors can try.

What does he think will impress them about the device?

A It offers them a range of different options.

B It gives them an alternative view of things.

C It provides them with a convincing experience.

7 You hear two students talking about some research on listening to music while studying.

What do they agree about?

A the effect of listening to music with lyrics

B the value of doing research into a subject like music

C the way lively music can motivate you to work hard

8 You hear a radio presenter talking about something that happens in space.

What is his aim?

A to give information about it

B to explain how scientists discovered it

C to encourage people to look out for it

→ p. 134 p. 135

Part 2

You will hear a girl called Alison giving a class presentation about a holiday she had on a traditional sailing ship. For questions **9–18**, complete the sentences with a word or short phrase.

Listening test audio

Holiday on a traditional sailing ship

Alison's holiday was paid for by an organisation that encourages young people's interest in

(9) ....

The ship's captain said that people he referred to as

(10) .... were not welcome on the ship.

Alison was worried that she might not have the

(11) .... required.

People on board the ship use the term **(12)** .... to mean a four-hour period of work.

The lack of **(13)** .... was the hardest thing for Alison to get used to.

Alison overcame her fear of **(14)** .... during the holiday.

Alison says that **(15)** .... was the most popular free-time activity on the ship.

Alison was disappointed to miss a **(16)** .... in a port where the ship stopped.

Alison wasn't expecting to see so many **(17)** .... when she was at sea.

Alison regretted not packing more **(18)** .... clothes for the voyage.

 → p. 134 p. 139

Part 3

You will hear five short extracts in which teenagers are talking about making a new friend. For questions **19–23**, choose from the list (**A–H**) what each speaker says. Use the letters only once. There are three extra letters which you do not need to use.

Listening test audio

A My first impressions of this person were wrong.

B I had often noticed this person before.

C We were introduced by a neighbour of mine.

D We became close because of a difficult shared experience.

E This person reminded me of someone else.

F We were surprised to discover we had several things in common.

G We'd been in touch before we actually met.

H I nearly caused this person a problem.

Speaker	Answer	Question
Speaker 1		**19**
Speaker 2		**20**
Speaker 3		**21**
Speaker 4		**22**
Speaker 5		**23**

→ p. 134 p. 141

Part 4

Listening test audio

You will hear an interview with a young man called Oliver Stanford, who is talking about how he became a professional gardener. For questions **24–30**, choose the best answer (**A**, **B** or **C**).

---

24 Oliver first became interested in his family's garden when

A he saw how his mother's work had transformed it.

B he was given complete responsibility for it.

C he realised that no one else really cared about it.

25 Once Oliver had decided to become a professional gardener, he was

A disappointed not to find an appropriate university course.

B surprised at the amount of work involved in the training.

C unwilling to request financial help from his parents.

26 What does Oliver say about his job at a garden centre?

A He was determined not to be put off by the physical hardships.

B He found seeing the results of his work there very rewarding.

C He felt it was the most valuable career preparation he could have.

27 Oliver was confident he could be a successful gardener because he had

A developed the necessary organisational skills.

B shown a talent for designing gardens that people liked.

C learnt a lot about plants from other gardeners.

28 What has Oliver found while working as a gardener in a city?

A It is difficult to get his equipment into people's gardens.

B The deadlines he has to work to are tight.

C His customers' expectations are unrealistic.

29 Oliver describes one gardening job he disliked, because he had to

A use plants that he knew weren't right for the soil.

B dig up plants that were home to wildlife.

C replace an area of grass with large stones.

30 What does Oliver particularly value about his work?

A turning an unattractive place into somewhere beautiful

B having the opportunity to work with other people

C earning enough money to have a small garden of his own

→ p. 134 p. 143

Test 4

READING AND USE OF ENGLISH (1 hour 15 minutes)

Part 1

For questions **1–8**, read the text below and decide which answer (**A**, **B**, **C** or **D**) best fits each gap. There is an example at the beginning (**0**).

Mark your answers on the separate answer sheet.

Example:

0 **A** exhausted **B** tired **C** unhappy **D** miserable

0	A ○	B ●	C ○	D ○

Slower melting ice cream

Are you **(0)** .... of trying to enjoy ice cream that melts more quickly than you can eat it? A new food ingredient may **(1)** .... an end to sticky hands gripping ice cream cones.

Scientists have discovered a protein that can be used to create ice cream that is more resistant to melting than **(2)** .... products. The protein binds the air, fat and water in ice cream, making it super-smooth.

The new ingredient could **(3)** .... ice creams to remain frozen for greater **(4)** .... of time in hot weather. The protein occurs naturally in some foods, and researchers have developed a method of producing it in the laboratory from sustainable **(5)** .... materials.

If the discovery lives up to the scientists' expectations, there would be a reduced **(6)** .... for ice cream manufacturers to deep freeze their products. **(7)** .... , they would not have to be kept so cold while being transported over long distances or when being **(8)** .... in shops or homes.

1	**A**	get	**B**	make	**C**	put	**D**	give
2	**A**	suitable	**B**	conventional	**C**	general	**D**	appropriate
3	**A**	enable	**B**	permit	**C**	entitle	**D**	oblige
4	**A**	ranges	**B**	lengths	**C**	extents	**D**	spaces
5	**A**	ready	**B**	key	**C**	raw	**D**	main
6	**A**	cause	**B**	demand	**C**	motive	**D**	request
7	**A**	Alternatively	**B**	Nevertheless	**C**	Admittedly	**D**	Furthermore
8	**A**	maintained	**B**	saved	**C**	reserved	**D**	stored

→ p. 145

Part 2

For questions **9–16**, read the text below and think of the word which best fits each gap. Use only **one** word in each gap. There is an example at the beginning (**0**).

Write your answers **IN CAPITAL LETTERS on the separate answer sheet.**

Example: | **0** | T | O |

How to photograph fish

My hobby is photographing fish and I always start my day early because that's when the fish begin **(0)** .... search for their food. I walk along the river bank to see **(9)** .... I can spot – I wear sunglasses which makes **(10)** .... easier for me to see any movement in the water. I've also bought a special lens for my camera, which **(11)** .... the same job as the sunglasses, so I can take quite good photos without getting wet.

However, to be close **(12)** .... to the fish to take really good photographs, I do **(13)** .... to get into the water. Fish can be curious and, as **(14)** .... as I keep very still, some of them will come right up to me. But after **(15)** .... while, I usually find my fingers are too cold to operate the camera! Once out of the water, I rush home to see **(16)** .... well my shots have turned out.

 → p. 145

Part 3

For questions **17–24**, read the text below. Use the word given in capitals at the end of some of the lines to form a word that fits in the gap **in the same line**. There is an example at the beginning (**0**).

Write your answers **IN CAPITAL LETTERS on the separate answer sheet.**

Example: | **0** | A | B | I | L | I | T | Y |

Our brains and technology

According to some psychologists, our **(0)** .... to **ABLE**
remember things is being negatively affected by our constant
use of electronic devices. Researchers claim that these devices
have almost become an **(17)** .... of our brains and **EXTEND**
that relying too **(18)** .... on them could possibly **HEAVY**
be **(19)** .... to us, because it can prevent the **HARM**
(20) .... of long-term memories. They say that the process of **DEVELOP**
recalling information can strengthen these memories, while at the same
time allowing our brains to forget other information that we no longer
need. And getting rid of this **(21)** .... information then makes **RELEVANT**
room in our brains for the storage of new facts and memories.

Although there's a **(22)** .... not to learn new facts, **TEMPT**
because we can always find any information we need online, there's
(23) .... that information obtained so easily is very quickly **EVIDENT**
forgotten. On the other hand, human brains are very good at adapting,
and after all, it would be **(24)** .... to expect people to ignore **REASON**
all the technology available nowadays.

→ p. 145

Part 4

For questions **25–30**, complete the second sentence so that it has a similar meaning to the first sentence, using the word given. **Do not change the word given.** You must use between **two** and **five** words, including the word given. Here is an example (**0**).

Example:

0 Prizes are given out when the school year finishes.

PLACE

Prize-giving .... end of the school year.

The gap can be filled by the words 'takes place at the', so you write:

Example:	**0**	*TAKES PLACE AT THE*

Write **only** the missing words **IN CAPITAL LETTERS on the separate answer sheet.**

---

25 Fran has got so many books there's no room left on this shelf!

TAKE

Fran's books .... the space on this shelf!

26 'Please don't tell Billy what I said!' Harry begged me.

ASKED

Harry .... Billy what he'd said.

27 In the class discussion, most students thought that school holidays should be longer.

FAVOUR

In the class discussion, most students .... school holidays being longer.

28 I decided not to go for a walk because it was too cold.

PUT

The cold weather .... going for a walk.

29 It really wasn't a good idea for Sally to mention the school team's poor performance in the football match.

BROUGHT

Sally really .... the school team's poor performance in the football match.

30 What a great film, we have to watch it again!

SUCH

It .... , we have to watch it again!

→ p. 145

Part 5

You are going to read an extract from an interview with a young actor, Peter Rose. For questions **31–36**, choose the answer (**A**, **B**, **C** or **D**) which you think fits best according to the text.

Mark your answers on the separate answer sheet.

Interview with a young actor

When I met Peter Rose, the young star of the new hit film, *The Ranger*, despite his striking looks and above average height, he appeared slightly embarrassed when we shook hands. He somehow lacked the confidence that might be expected from someone who is receiving so much praise. He spoke hesitantly, as if reluctant to express a strong opinion and possibly offend someone. Peter's a relatively new face in the acting world. As yet he hasn't had that many leading parts, but he's instantly recognisable. He leaves a lasting impression, even when playing minor parts, and he's skilled at suggesting in small and subtle ways the emotions of the characters he plays.

Peter took up acting as one of his many after-school activities; at the time, he would have said that his heart wasn't entirely in it and that his goal was to become a professional athlete. Aged 12, his natural ability as an actor became apparent when he made his debut in a professional play, but he didn't get carried away as so many other young actors do. Perhaps it was his cautious nature that distinguished him. He was wise enough to grasp how an acting career might develop, and how it might go wrong. As he began appearing in small roles he became increasingly worried about getting sucked into the celebrity rat race.

He took up a place at university with the intention of staying away from acting for a few years, and possibly permanently. 'As the demands of the course increased, I realised that my degree, although relevant and stimulating, wasn't in fact essential. Studying didn't seem to make sense any more. Although I dropped out after one year, college briefly served a purpose, putting my acting on hold and allowing me to reflect on whether I should fully commit to it,' Peter tells me.

His parents weren't too upset when he left college. 'They did suggest that I should do something as a backup, like a business course in case the acting career didn't work out, but both of them took the view that it wasn't an impossible dream,' Peter says. Celebrity continues to make him uneasy and he sends all his film memorabilia to his parents' house. He smiles when he says: 'I assumed all this stuff would go in a box in a cupboard, and only be looked at occasionally, but on a trip back home I discovered that it was all out on display. It's natural for parents to be satisfied when their children do well, but I'd really rather they were less enthusiastic about it.'

Before agreeing to appear in the new film *The Ranger*, Peter went through his customary process of questioning and analysis – in this case, reading the novel on which the film was based to see if the script did it justice. *line 6* 'It felt like the responsible thing to check the quality,' he says. 'I realised that the role was the challenge I'd been waiting for and I believed I had the technical skill.

In the new film, Peter stars alongside the famous actor George Schulman. While on set, did he turn to Schulman for professional advice? 'I wasn't sure that I should bother him with questions when we were filming.' He pauses and then adds: 'I'm yet to be persuaded of the use of looking up to role-models when you're an actor, because imitating the way other people portray characters isn't worthwhile in my view. I appreciated George's willingness to work incredibly hard and to give so much energy and passion to the film. And that's what I think is instructive, rather than any acting tips.'

31 The writer says that Peter's performances

A clearly reflect the personality he has.
B have failed to show what he is capable of.
C are memorable whatever the size of the role.
D tend to lack emotional depth.

32 What does the writer suggest made Peter unusual when he started acting?

A He was aware of the potential difficulties he might encounter.
B He had a natural talent that few young actors possess.
C He was distracted by the possibility of entering another profession.
D He believed he would be unable to achieve lasting success.

33 How does Peter feel about his time at university?

A annoyed that he wasn't able to learn anything useful
B satisfied that he tried his best to be successful
C guilty that he did not have the right priorities in life
D pleased that it provided an opportunity to think about his future

34 What does Peter say about his parents' attitude to his career?

A Their advice tends not to be helpful.
B They are keen to help him to protect his privacy.
C They doubt that it is a realistic choice in the long term.
D Their pride is expressed in a way that embarrasses him.

35 What does the writer mean by the phrase 'if the script did it justice' in line 61?

A if the script was too similar to the book
B if the script was as impressive as the book
C if the script avoided weaknesses in the book
D if the script made more demands than the book

36 What did Peter feel about working with George Schulman?

A disappointed that he failed to take advice from George
B frustrated at his inability to match George's acting skills
C unconvinced of the value of trying to copy George's style
D surprised at the way in which George treated him during filming

→ p. 145

Part 6

You are going to read an article about the way crocodiles sleep. Six sentences have been removed from the article. Choose from the sentences **A–G** the one which fits each gap (**37–42**). There is one extra sentence which you do not need to use.

Mark your answers on the separate answer sheet.

Crocodiles sleep with one eye open

Just in case any of you ever thought you could safely tiptoe past a sleeping crocodile, please reconsider – scientists have confirmed that the fearsome reptiles sleep with one eye open. Researchers in Australia and Germany have recently discovered that crocodiles, while dozing, can deploy what is called 'unilateral eye closure' to keep a lookout for potential threats, or spot animals they can hunt.

It is already known that birds, other reptiles and aquatic animals such as dolphins, seals and walruses have evolved 'unihemispheric' sleep, which is when one half of the brain stays awake while the other shuts down. This allows the animals to keep one eye open to monitor events around them. Researchers had believed for some time that crocodiles might be able to do so too. **37** ______ Now they have, and it lends significant weight to their theory.

Three juvenile saltwater crocodiles were taken from northern Queensland, Australia, to a large university aquarium and filmed 24 hours a day. Scientists confirmed that the crocodiles opened one eye during sleep in response to a mild stimulus. They asked a volunteer to stand still next to the aquarium for 10 minutes. **38** ______ Dr John Lesku, who led the study, said that after the volunteer had left the room they kept looking, through that one eye, at the place where he had last been standing.

A further experiment involved the researchers putting a new young crocodile in with the group. **39** ______ This was possibly because younger crocodiles are less able to defend themselves and need to be protected by the older members of the group.

Lesku said some of his colleagues in Germany had been doing similar experiments. **40** ______ 'It suggests that the crocodilian characteristic we have identified is not specific to one species,' he said. 'It persists into adulthood, meaning that an animal lying in wait to catch food could be perfectly still, yet at the same time be on the lookout for prey. If an animal went to the bank of a river, the crocodile could fully wake up and attack it. I would certainly never approach a crocodile whether its eyes are open or closed. A good rule is never to go anywhere near them.'

Further research is now being planned to monitor crocodiles' brain activity. **41** ______ That crocodiles should share characteristics with birds is not as surprising as some people might think. Birds are crocodiles' closest evolutionary relatives, having shared a common ancestor before splitting and becoming very different species about 155 million years ago.

Sleeping with one eye open may seem strange. **42** ______ 'We think that what birds and dolphins do seems unusual, but if it turns out that crocodiles and reptiles sleep in this way too, then it's the way *we* sleep that starts to look like the exception to the rule,' he said.

A They discovered that this behaviour was also present in adult Nile crocodiles and caimans.

B The animals responded to that quite strongly and watched the person closely with one eye open.

C As a result, it has been difficult to study this behaviour in the wild.

D But according to Lesku, it may be that land-based mammals, which completely shut down to sleep, are the exception.

E However, they had never had reliable evidence of this behaviour.

F This will aim to find out if one half does indeed shut down.

G Again, the crocodiles opened one eye and kept watch.

➔ p. 145

Part 7

You are going to read an article about four young people who are learning to cook. For questions **43–52**, choose from the people (**A–D**). The people may be chosen more than once.

Mark your answers on the separate answer sheet.

Which person

suggests that having an advisor available when things go wrong is very helpful?	**43**	
was determined to learn techniques through study after getting practical experience?	**44**	
compares cooking to another skill where variety is also essential for success?	**45**	
accepts that a family member has set a standard that they can't equal?	**46**	
has discovered that basic cookery skills have changed little over the years?	**47**	
records what happens when they use different cooking methods and ingredients?	**48**	
is aware that a family member disapproves of their source of information?	**49**	
has learnt through experimenting with a limited range of ingredients?	**50**	
relies more on experimentation than on following instructions closely?	**51**	
is grateful for the fact that they're not criticised for mistakes they make?	**52**	

 → p. 145

Learning to cook

A Billy

I've been having cookery classes at school, although I've somehow maintained an enthusiasm for making good food in spite of them! Luckily my mum, who's a pretty good cook herself, has always made my brother and me take turns in meal preparation, to ensure we learnt the essential skills. And those have been really useful for me in my classes, especially when we've had to improvise and make a meal using the very few things available to us there. That's really given me a good idea of what goes with what, and I'm much better at it now. And I've realised that to eat well, you have to learn how to cook well, and not just a few dishes either. Imagine you're a musician – people will get tired of hearing even a great song, if it's the only one you can play. That applies to cooking, too.

B Carolina

I've always enjoyed watching my mum throw a collection of unlikely foods together and produce something really delicious. And after being made to stick to recipes in school cookery classes I've come to the conclusion that they should be seen as loose guidelines, and just trying things out is what matters. So I generally avoid them, especially when I'm baking, and just making a note of what I've done and what I've used to do it can take me a lot further – a bit like in my science classes! Still, it's great having someone like my mum around to explain exactly why the fluffy sponge cake I was aiming for has turned out to be a flat pancake. I rarely find the answers to my questions in cookbooks or online, however hard I try. Despite all that I've learnt, though, I'll never measure up to my mum's natural ability – but at least she's given me a real love of good food.

C Matt

My mum says she's such a good cook because she's spent so many years cooking for all of us. But I reckon the fact that she was the eldest child in a large household is the real reason for it. I enjoy helping out in the kitchen, making easy stuff like pasta for everyone. But I often mess up, like the time I was put in total charge of dinner and I dished up the pasta way before I'd even started making the sauce! Anyway, having an understanding family that puts up with it all has given me the confidence to experiment further. A couple of months ago, I decided to get a better understanding of different basic skills by shutting myself in my room with a cookery book, only returning to the kitchen when I thought I could manage a few key recipes perfectly – which I could!

D Sarah

I had to be virtually dragged into the kitchen as a child to help out with getting meals on the table, so my mum certainly never imagined when I was young that I'd turn into an enthusiastic cook with some great recipes up my sleeve! But I'm always struck by how often I still make use of what I've learnt from her, whether that's making a soft sponge cake or making a little money go a long way. And I've realised for myself the value of great cookery books of the past – the methods written about in them are still used today. Mind you, my mum's horrified at the idea of me using a cookbook – unless it's one like hers, absolutely covered in her scribbled notes, and passed down through generations of our family!

WRITING (1 hour 20 minutes)

Part 1

You **must** answer this question. Write your answer in **140–190** words in an appropriate style on the separate answer sheet.

---

1 In your English class you have been talking about school holidays. Now your English teacher has asked you to write an essay.

Write your essay using **all** the notes and giving reasons for your point of view.

Some people say that the school holidays during the summer are far too long.

What do you think?

Notes

Write about:

1. forgetting what you've learnt

2. having time to relax

3. .... (your own idea)

 → p. 107

Part 2

Write an answer to **one** of the questions **2–4** in this part. Write your answer in **140–190** words in an appropriate style on the separate answer sheet. Put the question number in the box at the top of the answer sheet.

---

2 You receive this email from your English friend, Kim.

> Hi
>
> I'm writing to you because you always look so cool in the clothes you wear! I really love clothes too and want to be fashionable, but I don't have a lot of money to spend. Can you give me any advice or suggestions?
>
> I'm relying on you!
>
> Kim

Write your **email**.

3 You see this notice in an international magazine for teenagers.

> **Articles wanted**
>
> **Noisy or quiet?**
>
> We're looking for articles about the importance of noise and silence in teenagers' lives. Are you someone who prefers places to be noisy or quiet? Or does it depend on what you're doing?
>
> The best articles will appear in our magazine.

Write your **article**.

4 You have seen this announcement in an international magazine for teenagers.

> **Stories wanted**
>
> We are looking for stories for our new English-language magazine for teenagers. Your story must **begin** with this sentence:
>
> *Alex looked at the photograph in the newspaper and thought the people in it seemed very familiar.*
>
> Your story must include:
>
> - a phone call
> - a meeting

Write your **story**.

→ p. 108

LISTENING (approximately 40 minutes)

Listening test audio

Part 1

You will hear people talking in eight different situations.
For questions **1–8**, choose the best answer (**A**, **B** or **C**).

---

1 You hear a music teacher talking to members of a school choir.

What does she think they need to do to improve?

A show more enthusiasm when they are singing

B make sure they know the words to all the songs

C listen more carefully to other singers around them

2 You hear two friends discussing a presentation given by a writer.

What does the girl say about the presentation?

A It made her appreciate how hard a writer's life can be.

B It changed her ideas about how writers produce their work.

C It encouraged her to try out new ways of writing creatively.

3 You hear a girl talking about a cycle race she took part in.

She feels she didn't win because

A she'd done less training than usual.

B she'd been over-confident about her ability.

C she'd misjudged conditions along the route.

4 You hear a radio item about an art competition in South Korea.

As a result of the competition

A an unusual type of paint became widely used.

B local people began to appreciate public art.

C some artists achieved international fame.

5 You hear two friends talking about a teenage boy who won a surfing competition.

How do they both feel?

A surprised by his reaction to winning

B envious of the experience he's had

C impressed by his courage in taking part

6 You hear a man talking about a problem some turtles had trying to reach a wildlife park in Japan.

How was the problem solved?

A New accommodation was built for the turtles.

B An alternative route was found for the turtles.

C A temporary resting place was created for the turtles.

7 You hear a teacher telling his class about an 'environment day' the school is having.

In preparation for the day, the students should

A do online research to get ideas.

B develop the ideas they've already had.

C find ideas which will have a lasting effect.

8 You hear a man talking about an extreme marathon he took part in.

What was the hardest thing for him about the race?

A the possibility of failure

B the lack of practical support

C the challenging landscape

→ p. 146 p. 147

Part 2

You will hear a boy called Jake giving a class presentation about birdwatching, which is his hobby. For questions **9–18**, complete the sentences with a word or short phrase.

Listening test audio

Birdwatching

The place where Jake went birdwatching most recently was a

(9) .... in his local area.

Jake says that the **(10)** .... is the best time of year for birdwatching.

It was Jake's **(11)** .... who gave him the idea of writing a blog about birdwatching.

The name of Jake's blog is **(12)** ....

Jake compares an unusual bird he saw in Australia to a

(13) ....

Jake has seen a total of **(14)** .... different types of birds.

Jake says that recognising the **(15)** .... made by different birds is something he wants to get better at.

Jake recently built a **(16)** .... in his garden with his father.

Jake says that people should avoid giving **(17)** .... to birds.

To help him with his birdwatching, Jake hopes to get a

(18) .... soon.

 → p. 146 p. 151

Part 3

You will hear five short extracts in which members of a dance class are talking about preparing to take part in a dance show. For questions **19–23**, choose from the list (**A–H**) what each speaker says about their experience. Use the letters only once. There are three extra letters which you do not need to use.

Listening test audio

A My teacher inspired me to give a great performance.

B I discovered the value of teamwork.

C I was unable to cope with being physically uncomfortable.

D Being well prepared made me less nervous.

E I realised the importance of sharing my feelings with others.

F I recognised the need to be prepared for the unexpected.

G The concentration required was something I found hard.

H The contribution I made was appreciated by others.

Speaker 1		**19**
Speaker 2		**20**
Speaker 3		**21**
Speaker 4		**22**
Speaker 5		**23**

→ p. 146 p. 153

Part 4

You will hear an interview with a teenager called Tina Barker, who is talking about a local archaeology project she took part in last summer. For questions **24–30**, choose the best answer (**A**, **B** or **C**).

Listening test audio

---

24 Tina says the start of the project was delayed because they needed to

A get expert advice on where to begin digging.

B find the right kind of specialist equipment.

C gain permission from landowners.

25 What is Tina particularly hoping to discover about her village?

A evidence to support a theory she has about it

B the function of a key building in its history

C why people suddenly abandoned it

26 How did Tina feel when she dug up a wedding ring?

A disappointed to hear it wasn't made of something valuable

B pleased to find something that had been significant to its original owner

C keen to find out more about who it had once belonged to

27 What does Tina say about the archaeologist on site?

A He's very strict with the volunteers.

B He is frustrated by the attitude of the volunteers.

C He's keen to show the volunteers how to care for things they find.

28 Tina is concerned about the cows coming onto the site because

A the project could be badly affected by them.

B people seem unaware of the problems caused by them.

C excavated items are being destroyed by them.

29 What does Tina feel she's personally gained from the project?

A an ability to stay calm in difficult situations

B an awareness of the value of patience

C an appreciation of how local people once lived

30 Tina is keen that the items that have been found by her group should be

A sold to raise more money for another project.

B taken to major museums for a wider public to see.

C kept in the village to inform local people about their history.

→ p. 146 p. 155

Speaking tests

Test 1

Note: The visual material for Test 1 appears on pages 164–166.

Example Speaking test video

Part 1

2 minutes (3 minutes for groups of three)

Interlocutor

Good morning/afternoon/evening. My name is .... and this is my colleague, ...
And your names are?
Can I have your mark sheets, please?
Thank you.

First, we'd like to know something about you.

- Where are you from, *(Candidate A)*?
- And you, *(Candidate B)*?

Select one or more questions from any of the following categories, as appropriate.

Family and friends

- Do you prefer to spend time with your family or with your friends at the weekend? (Why?)
- Are there a lot of interesting things to do in your town at the weekend? (What do you do there?)
- Do you often have to do homework at the weekend? (How do you feel about that?)
- Can you tell us something about what you're planning to do next weekend?

Your interests

- Do you like to be busy every day? (Why? / Why not?)
- What sport do you enjoy playing? (Why do you like doing that?)
- Do you enjoy watching TV? (What's your favourite programme?) (Why do you like it?)
- Do you ever meet your friends in the evenings after school? (What do you do together?)

Future plans

- What are you going to do after school today? (Why?)
- What would you like to do for your next birthday? (Why?)
- Is there something you'd like to learn in the future? (What would you like to learn?) (Why?)
- What would you like to do when you leave school? (Why?)

Part 2

4 minutes (6 minutes for groups of three)

A Doing things together

Interlocutor	In this part of the test, I'm going to give each of you two photographs. I'd like you to talk about your photographs on your own for about a minute, and also to answer a question about your partner's photographs. *(Candidate A)*, it's your turn first. Here are your photographs. They show friends doing different things together. *Indicate the pictures on page 164 to the candidates.* I'd like you to compare the photographs, and say why you think the friends have decided to do these things together. All right?
Candidate A	*[1 minute.]*
Interlocutor	Thank you. *(Candidate B)*, which of these things would you prefer to do with your friends? (Why?)
Candidate B	*[Approximately 30 seconds.]*
Interlocutor	Thank you.

B Listening carefully in lessons

Interlocutor	Now, *(Candidate B)*, here are your photographs. They show students listening carefully in different lessons. *Indicate the pictures on page 165 to the candidates.* I'd like you to compare the photographs, and say why you think it might be important for the students to listen carefully in these lessons. All right?
Candidate B	*[1 minute.]*
Interlocutor	Thank you. *(Candidate A)*, which of these lessons would you prefer to have? (Why?)
Candidate B	*[Approximately 30 seconds.]*
Interlocutor	Thank you.

Part 3	4 minutes (5 minutes for groups of three)
Part 4	4 minutes (6 minutes for groups of three)

Part 3 Summer holidays away from home

Interlocutor	Now, I'd like you to talk about something together for about two minutes (*3 minutes for groups of three*). Some people think it's a good idea for teenagers to spend their summer holidays away from home, doing activities with other young people. Here are some of the things they think about and a question for you to discuss. First you have some time to look at the task. *Indicate the text on page 166 to the candidates. Allow 15 seconds.* Now, talk to each other about whether teenagers should spend their summer holidays away from home, doing activities with other young people.
Candidates	*[2 minutes (3 minutes for groups of three).]*
Interlocutor	Thank you. Now you have about a minute to decide what the best reason is for spending summer holidays away from home.
Candidates	*[1 minute (for pairs and groups of three).]*
Interlocutor	Thank you.

Part 4

Interlocutor

Use the following questions, in order, as appropriate:

- Have you ever been away from home during the summer holidays? (Where did you go? / What did you do?)
- Is it important for teenagers to spend time away from home? (Why? / Why not?)
- Do you think it's good for teenagers to go on holiday with their families? (Why? / Why not?)
- Some people think that students have too many holidays in the year. What do you think? (Why?)
- Some schools give students the chance to go on trips to other countries during the school year. Do you think this is a good idea? (Why? / Why not?)
- Is it important to do school work during the summer holidays? (Why? / Why not?)

Select any of the following prompts, as appropriate:

- What do you think?
- Do you agree?
- And you?

Thank you. That is the end of the test.

Test 2

Note: The visual material for Test 2 appears on pages 167–169.

Part 1
2 minutes (3 minutes for groups of three)

Interlocutor

Good morning/afternoon/evening. My name is .... and this is my colleague, ...
And your names are?
Can I have your mark sheets, please?
Thank you.

First, we'd like to know something about you.

- Where are you from, *(Candidate A)*?
- And you, *(Candidate B)*?

Select one or more questions from any of the following categories, as appropriate.

Family and friends

- Do you prefer to spend time with your family or with your friends at the weekend? (Why?)
- Are there a lot of interesting things to do in your town at the weekend? (What do you do there?)
- Do you often have to do homework at the weekend? (How do you feel about that?)
- Can you tell us something about what you're planning to do next weekend?

Your interests

- Do you like to be busy every day? (Why? / Why not?)
- What sport do you enjoy playing? (Why do you like doing that?)
- Do you enjoy watching TV? (What's your favourite programme?) (Why do you like it?)
- Do you ever meet your friends in the evenings after school? (What do you do together?)

Future plans

- What are you going to do after school today? (Why?)
- What would you like to do for your next birthday? (Why?)
- Is there something you'd like to learn in the future? (What would you like to learn?) (Why?)
- What would you like to do when you leave school? (Why?)

Part 2
4 minutes (6 minutes for groups of three)

A Eating in different places

Interlocutor	In this part of the test, I'm going to give each of you two photographs. I'd like you to talk about your photographs on your own for about a minute, and also to answer a question about your partner's photographs. *(Candidate A)*, it's your turn first. Here are your photographs. They show people eating in different places. *Indicate the pictures on page 167 to the candidates.* I'd like you to compare the photographs, and say what you think the people are enjoying about eating in these places. All right?
Candidate A	*[1 minute.]*
Interlocutor	Thank you. *(Candidate B)*, do you like having meals with your family? (Why?)
Candidate B	*[Approximately 30 seconds.]*
Interlocutor	Thank you.

B New activities

Interlocutor	Now, *(Candidate B)*, here are your photographs. They show people trying new activities. *Indicate the pictures on page 168 to the candidates.* I'd like you to compare the photographs, and say what you think the people might find difficult about these new activities. All right?
Candidate B	*[1 minute.]*
Interlocutor	Thank you. *(Candidate A)*, which of these activities would you like to try? (Why?)
Candidate B	*[Approximately 30 seconds.]*
Interlocutor	Thank you.

Part 3	4 minutes (5 minutes for groups of three)
Part 4	4 minutes (6 minutes for groups of three)

Part 3 Helping with homework

Interlocutor	Now, I'd like you to talk about something together for about two minutes (*3 minutes for groups of three*). Some people think that parents should help their children with their homework and other people disagree. Here are some of the things they think about and a question for you to discuss. First you have some time to look at the task. *Indicate the text on page 169 to the candidates. Allow 15 seconds.* Now, talk to each other about whether you think parents should help their children with their homework.
Candidates	*[2 minutes (3 minutes for groups of three).]*
Interlocutor	Thank you. Now you have about a minute to decide what the best reason is for parents not to help their children with their homework.
Candidates	*[1 minute (for pairs and groups of three).]*
Interlocutor	Thank you.

Part 4

Interlocutor

Use the following questions, in order, as appropriate:

- Some people say students spend too much time doing homework. Do you agree? (Why? / Why not?)
- Is it a good idea for students to do homework together? (Why? / Why not?)
- Should teachers give students homework to do during the school holidays? (Why? / Why not?)
- Some people think students shouldn't do any homework so that they can spend more time with their families. What do you think? (Why?)
- How important is it for families to find time to do things together? (Why?)
- Do you think students in (candidate's country) have enough free time to do what they want? (Why? / Why not?)

Select any of the following prompts, as appropriate:

- What do you think?
- Do you agree?
- And you?

Thank you. That is the end of the test.

Test 3

Note: The visual material for Test 3 appears on pages 170–172.

Part 1
2 minutes (3 minutes for groups of three)

Interlocutor

Good morning/afternoon/evening. My name is .... and this is my colleague, ...
And your names are?
Can I have your mark sheets, please?
Thank you.

First, we'd like to know something about you.

- Where are you from, *(Candidate A)*?
- And you, *(Candidate B)*?

Select one or more questions from any of the following categories, as appropriate.

Family and friends

- Do you prefer to spend time with your family or with your friends at the weekend? (Why?)
- Are there a lot of interesting things to do in your town at the weekend? (What do you do there?)
- Do you often have to do homework at the weekend? (How do you feel about that?)
- Can you tell us something about what you're planning to do next weekend?

Your interests

- Do you like to be busy every day? (Why? / Why not?)
- What sport do you enjoy playing? (Why do you like doing that?)
- Do you enjoy watching TV? (What's your favourite programme?) (Why do you like it?)
- Do you ever meet your friends in the evenings after school? (What do you do together?)

Future plans

- What are you going to do after school today? (Why?)
- What would you like to do for your next birthday? (Why?)
- Is there something you'd like to learn in the future? (What would you like to learn?) (Why?)
- What would you like to do when you leave school? (Why?)

Part 2

4 minutes (6 minutes for groups of three)

A Watching friends

Interlocutor	In this part of the test, I'm going to give each of you two photographs. I'd like you to talk about your photographs on your own for about a minute, and also to answer a question about your partner's photographs. *(Candidate A)*, it's your turn first. Here are your photographs. They show people watching their friends in different situations. *Indicate the pictures on page 170 to the candidates.* I'd like you to compare the photographs, and say why you think the people are watching their friends in these situations. All right?
Candidate A	*[1 minute.]*
Interlocutor	Thank you. *(Candidate B)*, would you like to do either of these things? (Why? / Why not?)
Candidate B	*[Approximately 30 seconds.]*
Interlocutor	Thank you.

B Summer afternoon

Interlocutor	Now, *(Candidate B)*, here are your photographs. They show people doing different things on a summer afternoon. *Indicate the pictures on page 171 to the candidates.* I'd like you to compare the photographs, and say what you think the people are enjoying about doing these things on a summer afternoon. All right?
Candidate B	*[1 minute.]*
Interlocutor	Thank you. *(Candidate A)*, which of these things would you prefer to do on a summer afternoon? (Why?)
Candidate B	*[Approximately 30 seconds.]*
Interlocutor	Thank you.

Part 3	4 minutes (5 minutes for groups of three)
Part 4	4 minutes (6 minutes for groups of three)

Part 3 Talent shows

Interlocutor	Now, I'd like you to talk about something together for about two minutes (*3 minutes for groups of three*). Some people think it's a good idea for teenagers to take part in talent shows and compete with other young people. Here are some of the things they think about and a question for you to discuss. First you have some time to look at the task. *Indicate the text on page 172 to the candidates. Allow 15 seconds.* Now, talk to each other about whether it's a good idea for teenagers to take part in talent shows and compete with other young people.
Candidates	*[2 minutes (3 minutes for groups of three).]*
Interlocutor	Thank you. Now you have about a minute to decide what the best reason is for teenagers not taking part in talent shows.
Candidates	*[1 minute (for pairs and groups of three).]*
Interlocutor	Thank you.

Part 4

Interlocutor

Use the following questions, in order, as appropriate:

- Have you ever taken part in a talent show? (What did you do? / How did you feel about it?)
- Is it better to be quite good at lots of different things or very good at one thing? (Why?)
- Some people say that children should never compete with each other. What do you think? (Why?)
- Some people say that children spend too much time learning new skills and should spend more time just playing together. What do you think? (Why?)
- Do you think it's true that anyone can be good at anything if they practise enough? (Why? / Why not?)
- Some people say you only really get better at anything if you have to compete with other people. What do you think? (Why?)

Select any of the following prompts, as appropriate:

- What do you think?
- Do you agree?
- And you?

Thank you. That is the end of the test.

Test 4

Note: The visual material for Test 4 appears on pages 173–175.

Part 1
2 minutes (3 minutes for groups of three)

Interlocutor

Good morning/afternoon/evening. My name is .... and this is my colleague, ...
And your names are?
Can I have your mark sheets, please?
Thank you.

First of all we'd like to know something about you.

- Where are you from, *(Candidate A)*?
- And you, *(Candidate B)*?

Select one or more questions from any of the following categories, as appropriate.

Your interests

- Do you like to be busy every day? (Why? / Why not?)
- What sport do you enjoy playing? (Why do you like doing that?)
- Do you enjoy watching TV? (What's your favourite programme?) (Why do you like it?)
- Do you ever meet your friends in the evenings after school? (What do you do together?)

Family and friends

- Do you prefer to spend time with your family or with your friends at the weekend? (Why?)
- Are there a lot of interesting things to do in your town at the weekend? (What do you do there?)
- Do you often have to do homework at the weekend? (How do you feel about that?)
- Can you tell us something about what you're planning to do next weekend?

Future plans

- What are you going to do after school today? (Why?)
- What would you like to do for your next birthday? (Why?)
- Is there something you'd like to learn in the future? (What would you like to learn?) (Why?)
- What would you like to do when you leave school? (Why?)

Part 2
4 minutes (6 minutes for groups of three)

A Competitions

Interlocutor	In this part of the test, I'm going to give each of you two photographs. I'd like you to talk about your photographs on your own for about a minute, and also to answer a question about your partner's photographs. *(Candidate A)*, it's your turn first. Here are your photographs. They show people taking part in different competitions. *Indicate the pictures on page 173 to the candidates.* I'd like you to compare the photographs, and say what you think the people are enjoying about taking part in these competitions. All right?
Candidate A	*[1 minute.]*
Interlocutor	Thank you. *(Candidate B)*, would you like to take part in either of these competitions? (Why? / Why not?)
Candidate B	*[Approximately 30 seconds.]*
Interlocutor	Thank you.

B Practising

Interlocutor	Now, *(Candidate B)*, here are your photographs. They show people practising different things. *Indicate the pictures on page 174 to the candidates.* I'd like you to compare the photographs, and say what you think the people might find difficult about practising these things. All right?
Candidate B	*[1 minute.]*
Interlocutor	Thank you. *(Candidate A)*, which of these things would you prefer to do? (Why?)
Candidate B	*[Approximately 30 seconds.]*
Interlocutor	Thank you.

Part 3	4 minutes (5 minutes for groups of three)
Part 4	4 minutes (6 minutes for groups of three)

Part 3 Spending pocket money

Interlocutor Now, I'd like you to talk about something together for about two minutes (*3 minutes for groups of three*).

Some people think children should be allowed to spend their pocket money in any way they want and other people disagree. Here are some of the things they think about and a question for you to discuss. First you have some time to look at the task.

Indicate the text on page 175 to the candidates. Allow 15 seconds.

Now, talk to each other about whether children should be allowed to spend their pocket money in any way they want.

Candidates *[2 minutes (3 minutes for groups of three).]*

Interlocutor Thank you. Now you have about a minute to decide the most important reason why children should be allowed to spend their pocket money in any way they want.

Candidates *[1 minute (for pairs and groups of three).]*

Interlocutor Thank you.

Part 4

Interlocutor Use the following questions, in order, as appropriate:

- Did you get pocket money when you were a child? (Did you prefer to save it or spend it? / Why?)
- Some people think children shouldn't have any pocket money at all. What do you think? (Why?)
- Some parents ask children to do jobs around the house to earn pocket money. Is this a good idea? (Why? / Why not?)
- Some people say that there should be no advertising on TV for children's toys and games because it makes children want to have too many things. What do you think? (Why?)
- Is it important for young people to try to save money? (Why? / Why not?)
- Do you think it's good for young people to get a part-time job while they're still at school so they can earn their own money? (Why? / Why not?)

Select any of the following prompts, as appropriate:

- What do you think?
- Do you agree?
- And you?

Thank you. That is the end of the test.

Sample Writing answers

Additional sample Writing answers in Resource bank

Sample A (Test 1, Question 1 – Essay)

Nowdays, people are too worried about the physical appearance of people and things. They would prefer the trending things and love to follow the steps of fashion. There are many factors that cause people too worried about how people and things look.

First of all, I would like to emphasize that human is the most sensitive animals in the world. They may get affected by the people or things nearby easily, especially friends. When they are admiring their friends, they will set their friends as a modal sample and follow exactly what they do. The main purpose is they just wanted to be like their friends.

The another factor is the effect of celebrities when they attend a celebrity, they will find out a crowd of people who decorated themselves with beautiful clothes or jewelly. Not only that, the design and decorate appliances will also attract them. This causes them try to copy or modify the identical things from what they had seen.

Last but not least, the social media is the main purpose that causes this problem. In the social media, we are able to acknowledge thousand of things. This will causes people start copying and following the things no social media, such as methods of dressing, methods of decorating something.

In a nut shell, I agree that we are too worried about how people and things look. This results the creativity of arselves has lost due to the factor of following the others. Therefore, we have to change our minds and become a real us without any identities with the others.

Subscale	Mark	Commentary
Content	5	All content is relevant to the task. The writer discusses physical appearance in relation to the two content points, stating that people *'wanted to be like their friends'* and celebrities inspire people to *'copy or modify the identical things form what they had seen'*. The writer also discusses their own idea, the effect social media has on people's appearance, in the fourth paragraph. The target reader is fully informed.
Communicative Achievement	3	The writer uses some of the conventions of an essay, such as an objective tone and a reasonably formal register, to communicate straightforward ideas. The format of the essay is clear and there is a clear introduction and conclusion, which sums up the writer's opinions, *'I agree that; Therefore, we have to…'*, as well as topic sentences which introduce the main idea in each paragraph. The target reader's attention is held.
Organisation	4	The essay is well organised and coherent. There is a clear structure to the text and each paragraph focuses on a specific point. There is a variety of linking words and cohesive devices used to connect the ideas across sentences and paragraphs, *'There are many factors; First of all; The another factor is; Not only that; Last but not least; In a nut shell; Therefore'*.

Language	2	There is a range of everyday vocabulary, including some colloquial phrases, which is related to the topic of fashion and appearance, '*trending; follow the steps of fashion; get affected by; admiring; decorated themselves with beautiful clothes or jewelly; In a nut shell; change our minds*'. However, some of the vocabulary choices make the meaning of some phrases difficult to understand, '*the design and decorate appliances will also attract them; we are able to acknowledge thousand of things*'. Simple grammatical structures are used with a good degree of control, for example present continuous forms, but there are errors when more complex ideas are attempted which require specific sentence structures, '*they will set their friends as modal sample; The another factor is the effect of celebrities when they attend a celebrity, they will find out a crowd of people who decorated themselves with*'. There are a number of noticeable errors with word choices and agreement, but meaning can usually still be determined.

Sample B (Test 1, Question 4 – Story)

Tom v/s Shark

It was Tom's first deep-sea diving lesson and he felt quite nervous. He dreamt about it his whole life and when we were about to jump into the sea he started asking questions. "What if I get lost? Will you rescue me?" he knew all the rules but I patiently answered all of them. Everything was going fine but Tom saw a shadow.

A big shadow of a very big shark. Tom didn't know how to warn the rest of the group because down there he couldn't scream. He forgot that and took his oxigen tube out of his mouth and began to swallow tons of water. I saw him and helped him to get into the boat.

Every time there is a beginner in the group, Max, the driver takes a photograph right after he or she gets out of the water. When Tom got out he started throwing up. In the photograph Tom has sea-plants coming out of his mouth and tears in his eyes.

I asked him what happened and I realized he imagined that shadow. I told him there were no sharks and started laughing. Seconds after, he wanted to do it again.

Subscale	Mark	Commentary
Content	5	All content is relevant to the task. The story begins with the prompt sentence and the content points are both included in a logical meaningful way. The target reader is fully informed.
Communicative Achievement	4	The writer uses the conventions of a narrative to tell the story in an effective way. There is some suspense, '*but Tom saw a shadow. A big shadow of a shark*', humour, '*In the photograph Tom has sea plants coming out of his mouth*', direct speech and a clear sequence of events which holds the target reader's attention, '*when we were about to jump into the sea he started; I saw him and helped him get into the boat; Seconds after, he wanted to do it again*'.
Organisation	4	The text is well organised and coherent. The story has a clear beginning, middle and an end and the events are presented in a logical sequence. There is a variety of linking words and cohesive devices, such as narrative tenses, used to connect the ideas through the text, '*he knew all the rules but I patiently answered; because down there he couldn't scream. He forgot that; Max, the driver takes a photograph … In the photograph*'.
Language	4	There is a range of vocabulary related to the sea and diving, which is used appropriately, '*jump into the sea; warn; oxigen tube; swallow tons of water; boat; beginner; throwing up; realized he imagined*'. There is a range of simple and some complex grammatical forms, mainly simple past and present tenses, but these are used with a good degree of control, '*Everytime … throwing up*'. There are very few errors, but there are occasions where different tenses, such as past perfect, would be more appropriate, '*He dreamt about it his whole life; I asked him what happened; realized he imagined*'.

Sample C (Test 2, Question 1 – Essay)

Many people suppose that students should help to make decisions about what happens at school. Personally, I believe that students must have an opportunity to take part in school life.

At first, they may decide which subjects to study they need. If students have different interests, why they should learn the same subjects. If you are learning something that you don't like, it is just wasting of time.

At the second, some of school rules can be also created by students. Of course, it is not possible to allow pupils adopt all the rules without discussing it with administration. They must have a discussion and reach a compromise.

As for me, I think that students can choose the food which they will eat. It can be even lobster, if they want.

In conclusion, I want to say that undergrads must help the director to create some ideas to do the school life better.

Subscale	Mark	Commentary
Content	5	All content is relevant. The writer discusses the two content points, school subjects and school rules, and their own idea involves allowing schoolchildren to '*choose the food which they will eat*'. The target reader is fully informed.
Communicative Achievement	3	The writer uses some of the conventions of the essay genre. There is an introduction to the topic, a brief discussion of each aspect and a conclusion. The tone and register of the text is appropriate and there is a combination of personal and more general ideas, '*Personally, I believe; it is not possible to allow; As for me, I think*'. Straightforward ideas are communicated and the target reader's attention is held.
Organisation	2	The text is generally well organised and coherent. There is some attempt to structure the information throughout the whole text, '*At first; At the second; As for me; In conclusion*', but the individual sentences appear to be unconnected at times, due to the limited number of cohesive devices and some difficulties with some sentence structures, '*they may decide which subjects to study they need. If students have different interests … If you are learning something; I think that students can choose the food which they will eat. It can be even lobster*'.
Language	3	There is a range of everyday vocabulary, which is suitable for the task, and which is used appropriately. Some less common lexis is also attempted, '*must have an opportunity; different interests; wasting of time; created; adopt all the rules; administration; reach a compromise; lobster; undergrads*'. The writer uses a range of simple and some complex grammatical forms with a good degree of control, '*must have an opportunity to take part in; can also be created; without discussing*'. There are some errors with word choices word order and agreement, but these do not impede communication, '*which subjects to study they need; wasting of time; some of school rules; adopt all the rules without discussing it; it can be even lobster*'.

Sample D (Test 2, Question 4 – Email)

Hi mel,

It's been ages since the last time I heard from you. How is your family? I'm sorry to hear that Chris isn't returning the things to borrow to him. I think you should definetely talk to him and tell him how you feel, maybe he hasn't realised what he's doing. Besides, I think that honesty is one of the fundamental values to have if you want to mantain a healthy friendship. Although it could be a a little bit awkard, talking to him can help him become, in some way, a better and more responsible person.

Hey, I almost forgot, I'm having a birthday party next month and it'd be amazing if you could come. I guess it's time for me to get on with the study I've been avoiding. I look forward to hearing from you again, let me know how did it go with Chris.

Best wishes,
Sofi

Subscale	Mark	Commentary
Content	5	All content is relevant to the task. The writer offers appropriate advice to the reader about their problem with Chris, '*I think you should definetely talk to him and tell him how you feel*', and suggests how this may help. Although the second paragraph is not directly related to the problem, it reinforces the fact the two people have a friendly relationship. The target reader is fully informed.
Communicative Achievement	3	The tone of the email is friendly and there is a consistently informal register, which holds the target reader's attention, '*It's been ages since the last time I heard from you; I'm sorry to hear that; Hey, I almost forgot; It'd be amazing if you could come*'. The writer expresses straightforward ideas and includes some appropriate functional language to express advice and solutions to a problem, '*I think you should; maybe he hasn't realised; talking to him can help; let me know how did it go with Chris*'.
Organisation	3	The text is generally well organised and coherent. The email uses appropriate opening and closing phrases, '*Hi mel; It's been ages since; Hey, I almost forgot; Best wishes*', as well as suitable linking words and cohesive devices throughout the text, '*talk to him and tell him; Besides; Although; Hey*'.
Language	3	There is a range of everyday vocabulary which is used appropriately to express the writer's ideas, '*realised; honesty; fundamental values; healthy friendship; responsible; avoiding*'. There is a range of simple and some complex grammatical forms, such as a variety of verb tenses and accurate use of prepositions, '*It's been ages since the last time I heard from you; maybe he hasn't realised what he's doing; Although it could be; talking to him can help him become; I'm having…and it'd be amazing; the study I've been avoiding*'. There are a few errors, but they do not impede communication, '*the things to borrow to him; mantain; awkard; how did it go*'.

Sample E (Test 3, Question 1 – Essay)

Nowadays, is more common to go somewhere alone because most of us are always connected with our mobile phone. Because of that, is why I think we don't go anywhere alone.

In my point of view, there are some activities that you can enjoy more going alone like going to the mountain or running because they provide you peaceful and time to think in your own ideas.

Althoug there are other times that we need to stay with people and socialice. A good way to practice this, I think is going shopping with your friends because is not only buying, is having a good time, talking, smiling or hugging them.

Despite the fact we need to feel love, staying with friends or family meanwhile you have to study is not a good idea because you cannot concentrated as well as staying alone.

To sum up, we should decided about what activities we can do better alone and which not. Nobody can tell you.

Subscale	Mark	Commentary
Content	5	All content is relevant to the task. The writer discusses the content points, claiming that going shopping is better to do with friends, while studying is best done alone, '*you cannot concentrated as well as staying alone*'. The writer's own idea involves doing activities on your own, such as running or hiking, as '*they provide you peaceful and time to think*'. The target reader is fully informed.
Communicative Achievement	3	The writer uses some of the conventions of an essay, such as an introduction and a conclusion as well as a semi-formal register to communicate straightforward ideas. The writer gives their own opinions about the topic in a balanced way, which helps to hold the target reader's attention, '*In my point of view; there are other times that we need; A good way to practice this, I think; Despite the fact*'.
Organisation	3	The text is generally well organised and coherent. The text is separated into paragraphs, each one focusing on a different idea and appropriate cohesive devices and linking words are used to compare and contrast ideas across the paragraphs and through the text, '*Nowadays; Because of that; In my point of view; Althoug; to practice this; Despite the fact; To sum up*'.
Language	2	The writer uses a range of everyday vocabulary, including some accurate collocations to express their ideas, '*enjoy more; going to the mountain or running; time to think; talking, smiling or hugging; need to feel love*'. Simple grammatical forms are used with a good degree of control, but there are some clauses which are missing a subject, '*because is not only buying*'. There are many errors, particularly when trying to use more complex structures, or when trying to express more complex ideas, '*they provide you peaceful; staying with friends and family meanwhile you have to study; you cannot concentrated; we should decided*'.

Sample F (Test 3, Question 2 – Review)

Zootopia is a movie about a society run by animals and a bunny who wants to be become the first bunny cop. Together with a fox she has to solve a missing mammal case in 48 hours.

Despite how incredibly silly that sounds Zootopia actually tackles some very mature themes. There is a lot of, not always that subtle, commentary on racism which is handled really well for a kids movie. The animation is also stellar and overall it's just a fun buddy cop mystery. With some great laughs.

The world building and atmosphere really engrosses you into the film even more. It's very technically impressive. Since it's a cgi animated movie they had to model every single back ground character and they did an excellent job. They all look unique which adds to the overall presentation of the film.

In concept this movie may seem silly but it nails it in the execution. Although it's a "kids" movie it's still suited and interesting for adults. Therefore I strongly recommend it.

Subscale	Mark	Commentary
Content	5	All content is relevant to the task. The writer gives some factual information about the film, tells the reader what they think about it and gives a clear recommendation at the end. The target reader is fully informed.
Communicative Achievement	5	The conventions of a review, such as writing objectively and informatively in an engaging way, are used effectively to communicate complex ideas, particularly when discussing the themes of the film, '*Despite how incredibly silly that sounds Zootopia actually tackles some very mature themes; There is a lot of … commentary on racism which is handled really well; In concept this movie may seem silly but it nails it in the execution*'. The target reader's attention is held throughout and they would be able to decide if the film would appeal to them or not.
Organisation	5	The text is well organised and coherent. There is a variety of cohesive devices and some more complex organisational features, such as relative clauses, ellipsis and forward and backward referencing, which are used to generally good effect, '*and a bunny who wants to become; Together with a fox, she has to solve; Despite how incredibly silly that sounds; There is a lot of, not always that subtle, commentary; which adds to; Although it's a "kids" movie, it's still suited … for adults*'.
Language	5	There is a range of vocabulary, including collocated phrases, related to film and cinema, which is used appropriately and to good effect, '*solve a missing mammal case; incredibly silly; tackles some very mature themes; subtle; commentary on racism; handled; stellar; fun buddy cop mystery; technically impressive; background character; unique; Concept; execution*'. The writer demonstrates control over a range of grammatical forms, such as control over the past and present tenses when describing how the film was made and what the film is about. The sentences are well constructed and although there are a few errors, these are due to ambition and attempting to use more complex language, '*word building; really engrosses you*'.

Sample G (Test 4, Question 1 – Essay)

Some people say that the school holidays during the summer are far too long. On the one hand, find these words quite right. Past 3 months of holidays, when you come back to the school, it's hard to start learning first weeks. It's just because of that you are forgetting what you've learnt last school year.

On the other hand, I'm entirely disagree with it. I don't have enough time to relax, as of 2 of 3 months I'm working to earn money to go travel in the last 3rd month. Also, in Estonia we have very good weather not only in summer but in the last month of spring and beginning of autumn too. I feel really sad when I'm studying and outside is good weather.

I think that government should watch this question and for example make school days a bit shorter in good weather. Like one idea more, classes can be outside. As I'm a student, a lot of teenagers will be agree with me.

Subscale	Mark	Commentary
Content	5	All content is relevant to the task. The writer discusses the main question and gives their own opinion on whether they think school summer holidays are too long in relation to the two content points, forgetting what you've learnt and having time to relax. The writer's own idea involves adapting the school day according to the weather. The target reader is fully informed.
Communicative Achievement	3	The writer uses an appropriate tone and register to communicate straightforward ideas. The essay contains an introduction and a conclusion and although it is mainly the writer's own views which are communicated, there is a suggestion that these views would be welcomed by others, '*As I'm a student, a lot of teenagers will be agree with me'.* Although there are a few errors, the target reader's attention is held throughout the text.
Organisation	3	The text is generally well organised and coherent. The essay is divided into paragraphs and each one focuses on a separate idea, learning, working and relaxing and the length of the school day. There is a variety of linking words and simple cohesive devices are used to connect the ideas through the text, '*On the one hand; because of that; On the other hand; Also; not only in summer but in the last month of spring; and for example*'.
Language	2	There is a range of everyday vocabulary which is used appropriately to express the writer's ideas, '*entirely disagree; earn money; good weather; spring; autumn; government; a bit shorter*', although some of the vocabulary is repeated from the input material. The writer uses simple expressions and grammatical structures with a good degree of control, such as simple present tenses. However, there are a number of errors with word order and word choices when trying to express certain ideas, '*find these words quite right; Past 3 months of holidays; to go travel; should watch this question; Like one idea more*'.

Sample H (Test 4, Question 3 – Article)

It depends on what I'm doing, but most of the time I prefer places to be noisy because I'm noisy too. For example, in school during lessons, I like to talk with my friends rather than work on my own.

However, sometimes I do like to work on my own, but that's a rare situation. This happens when I'm not on schedule. It's the pressure to be on schedule again that makes me want to work on my own.

Then, when I'm on schedule again, I like it to be noisy again and start talking to my friends. Now it sounds like I always start the noise, but that isn't true. I start talking when it already is a bit noisy, not when everyone around me is working in silence.

Apart from school, it also depends on the situation whether I like it to be noisy or quiet. When I'm in the open nature and hear birds singing, I like to hear the birds, but I don't like it to be noisy then.

Subscale	Mark	Commentary
Content	5	All content is relevant to the task. The writer discusses when they like to be in noisy places and quiet places and why, '*sometimes I do like to work on my own…This happens when I'm not on schedule; when I'm on schedule again, I like it to be noisy*'. Although the writer focuses on when they like to be quiet or noisy, there is still some reference to a specific place, '*school during lessons; open nature*'. The target reader is fully informed.
Communicative Achievement	3	The writer uses some of the features of an article, such as describing personal preferences and using a fairly neutral tone, to communicate straightforward ideas, '*It depends on what I'm doing; Now it sounds like I always start the noise, but that isn't true*'. The target reader's attention is held due to the picture which is built up of the writer, '*I prefer places to be noisy because I'm noisy too; It's the pressure to be on schedule again that makes me want to work on my own; I like to hear the birds, but I don't like it to be noisy then*'.
Organisation	3	The text is generally well organised and coherent. Although there isn't a clear introductory statement, the topic is clearly stated in the first paragraph. There is a variety of linking words and some cohesive devices used to connect the ideas through the text, '*but; because; For example; rather than; However; This; Then; and; Apart from school; also*'.
Language	3	The writer uses a range of everyday vocabulary related to the topic of noisy places appropriately, '*rare situation; schedule; pressure; silence; open nature*'. The grammatical forms and structures are used with a good degree of control, particularly when providing examples or extra information or comparing and contrasting information, '*It depends on what I'm doing, but most of the time I prefer places to be noisy because I'm noisy too; I like to talk with my friends rather than work on my own; It's the pressure to be on schedule again that makes me want to work on my own; I start talking when it already is a bit noisy, not when everyone around me is working in silence*'. There are very few errors in the text.

Test 1 answer key

Reading and Use of English

Answer key with extra explanations in Resource bank

Part 1

1 B **2** A **3** B **4** D **5** B **6** C **7** A **8** C

Part 2

9 from **10** there **11** being **12** as **13** on **14** of
15 few **16** to

Part 3

17 amusement **18** underground **19** accidentally **20** anxiety
21 shortage **22** relief **23** researchers **24** exploration

Part 4

25 so ABSORBED | by/in (reading)
26 IF (only) we | 'd/had left
27 is/'s /will be/'ll be CAPABLE of | solving
28 as/so LONG as | you take
29 was not/wasn't WILLING | to help
30 was DETERMINED | she would go/she'd go/to go

Part 5

31 D **32** C **33** A **34** B **35** D **36** C

Part 6

37 F **38** C **39** G **40** B **41** E **42** A

Part 7

43 C **44** B **45** D **46** A **47** C **48** D **49** C **50** B **51** D **52** A

Listening

Answer key with extra explanations in Resource bank

Part 1

1 A **2** B **3** B **4** A **5** A **6** A **7** C **8** A

Part 2

9 animation **10** physics **11** round **12** crocodile
13 drawings **14** visitors **15** sound(s) **16** dinosaur
17 football stadium **18** dimensions

Part 3

19 E **20** D **21** H **22** C **23** B

Part 4

24 B **25** C **26** B **27** A **28** C **29** A **30** B

Audioscript

Test One.

I am going to give you the instructions for this test. I shall introduce each part of the test and give you time to look at the questions. At the start of each piece you will hear this sound:

tone

You will hear each piece twice.

Remember, while you are listening, write your answers on the question paper. You will have five minutes at the end of the test to copy your answers onto the separate answer sheet.

There will now be a pause. Please ask any questions now, because you must not speak during the test.

[pause]

Now open your question paper and look at Part One.

[pause]

PART 1 *You will hear people talking in eight different situations. For questions 1 to 8, choose the best answer (A, B or C).*

Question 1 *You hear two students discussing some research into the behaviour of fish.*

[pause]

tone

Boy: What are you reading, Josie?

Girl: An article about some new research. Apparently, some scientists decided to try and find out if fish could recognise different people's faces.

Boy: That's a funny topic to choose! Surely fish can't do that!

Girl: Oh, I dunno. I've always felt my goldfish can tell the difference between me and my brother.

Boy: That sounds unlikely. But what did the researchers actually discover?

Girl: Well, they claim to have found that the fish learnt to identify specific faces of the people who fed them. But don't ask me how they went about proving that – it sounded very complicated. And, I'm not entirely sure whether it's a serious bit of work or not.

[pause]

tone

[The recording is repeated.]

[pause]

Question 2 *You hear a boy telling his friend about an important football match he will play in soon.*

[pause]

tone

Girl: It's your big match next week, isn't it?

Boy: Yeah – and I'm not looking forward to it. The other team's really strong. And to be honest, I hate playing in midfield.

Girl: But you did well in your last match.

Boy: I'm better as a striker, though. I might see if the coach would swap me.

Girl: It's too close to the match now. You could always ask him to fit in more training this week.

Boy: I don't think there's any choice, is there? I'll do that. I was going to suggest that James in our class could play – he's brilliant – he doesn't think he can it make though.

[pause]

tone

[The recording is repeated.]

[pause]

Question 3 *You hear two friends talking about a rock band.*

[pause]

tone

Boy: Have you heard about that band, The Comets? Apparently they've split up.

Girl: People are saying online that they all disagree about what musical direction to take – some want to do heavy rock, others prefer pop stuff.

Boy: They're just rumours and gossip, if you ask me. There are some strong personalities in the band, though. They were bound to fall out eventually.

Girl: Well, that's what seems to happen with most bands, isn't it?

Boy: Just overdoing it might be a factor, you know. They probably burnt themselves out.

Girl: I suppose that is a reason why many bands split. Look at the facts, though – they've only done two concerts in the last year.

[pause]

tone

[The recording is repeated.]

[pause]

Question 4 *You hear a teacher talking to his class after a discussion on space exploration.*

[pause]

tone

Man: During the class discussion we had today many of you expressed the opinion that space exploration is a huge waste of money. You put forward the argument that we can't afford it when we have so many problems on Earth that need tackling first. That makes sense on the face of it and you certainly had a good discussion. But of course one of the problems we're likely to have one day is lack of resources – particularly minerals. On other planets in the solar system we might be able to locate and extract such minerals. Therefore all the money spent now may well turn out to be worthwhile in the long run.

[pause]

tone

[The recording is repeated.]

[pause]

Question 5 *You hear two friends talking about a riverboat trip they've been on.*

[pause]

tone

Girl: Did you enjoy the boat trip?

Boy: Yeah. It was great to see the city from the river, wasn't it?

Girl: I've done that trip once before and the buildings are pretty amazing – no more than when you're looking at them from the bank, though really. What I didn't get last time was an explanation of what I was looking at – I appreciated that.

Boy: Normally I'm not a fan of commentaries over loud speakers but it added something to the trip.

Girl: And then having music played as we travelled down the river at night made it really cool.

Boy: It was a fantastic evening anyway, so that didn't really make any difference to me.

[pause]

tone

[The recording is repeated.]

[pause]

Question 6 *You hear a boy talking about working as a volunteer in a nature reserve.*

[pause]

tone

Boy: Last summer I worked as a volunteer in a nature reserve. I'd often been there when I was younger and was keen to let everyone see what I'd learnt about the place. I didn't know what to expect, but obviously I never thought we'd be given a whole list of easy options. And I was right. I was given some gardening jobs – not really my thing as I've always thought of gardening as pretty dull and for old people. It turned out, though, that I actually managed to make a difference to the place and it was cool just standing back and having a look at what I'd done.

[pause]

tone

[The recording is repeated.]

[pause]

Question 7 — *You hear a radio news item about National Ice Cream Month in the USA.*

[pause]

tone

Woman: Ice cream is the USA's favourite dessert. So much so that in 1984 the country's then president made July 'National Ice Cream Month', and the third Sunday of that month 'National Ice Cream Day'. All Americans are supposed to celebrate by eating lots of ice cream. If they're concerned about the calories involved, there are plenty of low-calorie ice creams available. And this year a leading US ice cream manufacturer is marking the month by adding a new flavour to its repertoire each week. People can also celebrate the occasion by purchasing a set of five stamps produced by the post office, each with a picture of a different ice cream on it.

[pause]

tone

[The recording is repeated.]

[pause]

Question 8 — *You hear a girl talking about a science project she did at school.*

[pause]

tone

Girl: Last term our science teacher put us into groups to do a project – our group had to look at how people learn and remember things. We spent ages working out ways to test different learning styles. Students in other groups were keen to find out what sort of learners they were – then I tested myself. My results showed I learnt best by listening to information first without trying to write anything down. I've never been any good at languages – so I tried that out in my Spanish classes – and it did seem to work! Although it did take time to get used to learning things in a new way.

[pause]

tone

[The recording is repeated.]

[pause]

That is the end of Part One.

Now turn to Part Two.

[pause]

PART 2

You will hear a man called Ben Gardener talking about his job, making large models from plastic building blocks. For questions 9 to 18, complete the sentences with a word or short phrase.

You now have forty-five seconds to look at Part Two.

[pause]

tone

Hi! I'm Ben Gardener, here to tell you about my unusual job! You may have played with plastic building bricks when you were younger? Well, I now use bricks just like those to make models for a special theme park. People go there to see the models, as well as to go on the rides.

How did I get this job? Well, I'd already had several jobs in theme parks. I'd worked in plumbing, repairing things like the fountains and water slides there. And I'd also had a job as an engineer, where I worked in animation – getting large models to move and look lifelike.

To get work like mine, it's also important to have qualifications in certain subjects, like design to help with the model building itself, and art, for creative ideas to make more interesting new rides. My degree in physics has helped me understand important things like speed on the rides and the forces involved.

When I applied to work at the theme park, I attended a selection day. I had to demonstrate I could make models from plastic bricks. They're obviously square or rectangular. I had no problem building trucks, robots – objects like that, even star shapes weren't too tricky. One task, though, was to produce something round – a head, or the moon – something like that. It was tough!

Later we had to make a more complex model that we'd planned beforehand. We'd been shown things that had been done before – a house with furniture, and one I thought was great – a racing car complete with driver. I decided on a crocodile, which they must have liked because it got me the job! I was more impressed by someone who'd built a giraffe. Spectacular!

Now I'm actually doing the job, I've found the design stage is very important. I'm always at my desk, which is covered with pieces of graph paper, for making plans of models, and loads of pencils, all different thicknesses. And then my drawings – nothing's more important than those, cos obviously they form the basis of the design. I also have several cameras to take photos I need for background information.

The plastic bricks I use to make my models all clip together by themselves, but I use glue as well, to actually stick the bricks into place. They're permanently outside so they're designed not to be affected by the weather. But they do get a lot of handling by visitors, so it's really vital to do this if the models are going to stay in one piece!

Recently I've been asked to use the experience I'd gained working at other theme parks to design models which move. I work with the team that's doing the installation of a new model. That means I sort out things like the electrical controls, how to use lighting effectively for atmosphere, and I create the sounds the model will make – that's the most thrilling bit for me – just experimenting.

Some models I've made have problems. I remember one of a horse, which took six of us to put into position. And another of a dinosaur was tricky – it was already built, but had to be made safe by tightening screws from the inside – a job that I was given. And I've had positive comments about the model of a whale I made – mainly about the size of it!

And new projects? Well, I'm into model buildings now – all made out of bricks, like an incredibly tall tower. And one I'm particularly proud of – a model castle, which people say is very realistic. I've now been asked to make a football stadium, including changing rooms and refreshment stands – that could be quite problematic!

Anyway, whenever I'm working on a building, I need to see an example of the real thing. I use the internet, but I need an accurate idea of the dimensions of the place, and the only reliable way to get that is visit it. And while I'm there, I also get the impression of the atmosphere of the place, and see the details – all aspects of my design.

So ... any questions?

[pause]

Now you will hear Part Two again.

tone

[The recording is repeated.]

[pause]

That is the end of Part Two.

Now turn to Part Three.

[pause]

PART 3

You will hear five short extracts in which teenagers are talking about their experience of speaking in public. For questions 19 to 23, choose from the list (A to H) what each speaker felt about the experience. Use the letters only once. There are three extra letters which you do not need to use.

You now have thirty seconds to look at Part Three.

[pause]

tone

Speaker 1

In my geography class we spent a week giving class presentations. Unfortunately I hadn't checked what topics other people were doing as we were supposed to. Then one of my classmates did virtually the same presentation I was going to do – I'd spent a long time preparing it and was very pleased I'd got it all done in time. Now I had no choice but to talk about something else and felt a bit uncomfortable having to explain to my teacher what had happened. Some presentations were quite impressive. It motivated me to do my best, even though I did the second one without any preparation. Anyway, people were quite complimentary, which was something.

[pause]

Speaker 2

I was a member of the school debating society and we entered a competition against some other schools. When my turn came to speak I know I must've sounded and looked very nervous, but it was the same for everyone, I guess. Anyway, I'm glad to say I got through it without slipping up or forgetting key facts. I really felt I could've done more thorough research, even though I spent ages on it. My sister had tried to be helpful because she'd done a similar project last year, so I couldn't really tell her I was managing okay without her. Anyway, the main thing was my school won the competition!

[pause]

Speaker 3

I gave a short speech in front of the whole school at our annual prize day. I'd expected to be nervous and sure enough I was, despite all the encouragement from my class teacher. I didn't actually take any of the advice I was offered. I was too busy endlessly rehearsing in front of the mirror. I just thought that repeating it would pay off. Oh well, my pretty average performance was quickly forgotten as it turned out. Nobody commented on it at all, in fact, because one of the teachers made a brilliant speech straight after me and that's all anyone talked about, and fair enough – it was very funny.

[pause]

Speaker 4

I was interviewed live on TV about playing football, because I'd just won an award. I was given plenty of time to think carefully about what I was going to say and make some notes, but it still wasn't enough. The interviewer ran through the questions with me in advance. I just switched off though so that wasn't helpful. I was just in a panic and wasn't able to calm down – it was a shame and I was cross with myself because I've always wanted to be on TV. Friends and relatives were really nice afterwards, saying I came across well but I didn't listen – I know it wasn't true.

[pause]

Speaker 5

[pause]

We had a class discussion last week. I've got some very clever, confident classmates, and I felt I had to make a reasonable contribution. It wasn't a formal debate so I tried talking without notes, but it was difficult to avoid getting things wrong doing that. It was only my class so I shouldn't have felt nervous – I still did though when it came to it. <u>And I found I didn't need all the research I'd done, but still thought it was an achievement to have covered as much as I did.</u> Our teacher is usually very helpful – giving us notes and things. This time he left us to cope on our own though.

[pause]

Now you will hear Part Three again.

tone

[The recording is repeated.]

[pause]

That is the end of Part Three.

Now turn to Part Four.

[pause]

PART 4 *You will hear an interview with a student called Laura Benson, who is talking about her experience of studying caterpillars and other insects in a rainforest in Central America. For questions 24 to 30, choose the best answer (A, B or C).*

You now have one minute to look at Part Four.

[pause]

tone

Interviewer: Laura Benson and nine other students recently spent three weeks in a rainforest in Costa Rica in Central America. They were there to help some scientists carry out a study of insects. Laura have you ever been anywhere like that before?

Laura: We have forests in Scotland where I'm from, so I had an idea what being surrounded by trees was like – there are so many incredible shades of green. In Scotland, though, forests are peaceful places, whereas in Costa Rica they're totally the opposite – full of insects, parrots and other wildlife all calling out to each other. That's what really struck me when I got there. It was over thirty degrees centigrade and extremely humid, but I knew Costa Rica was tropical.

Interviewer: As I understand it, the scientists were studying varieties of butterflies and the caterpillars that turn into those butterflies. Were you involved in collecting caterpillars for them?

Laura: Yes. There are hundreds of different kinds of caterpillars there – thin, fat, smooth, hairy … some look like the leaves around them. The scientists knew exactly where to find them – they'd spot half-eaten leaves and the caterpillars would be there. I didn't have those skills, though. I had to crawl around searching under plants. I used a special scoop tool to pick caterpillars up – that was to avoid damaging them rather than any fear of touching insects.

Interviewer: Did you help the scientists in other ways?

Laura: Yes. I helped a Mexican biologist called Ana. She was researching various caterpillars, from tiny ones, to some huge ones the size of your finger. They'd be on a leaf eating it – you know, having dinner – and she'd push them with a stick to see how they'd react. The idea was to find out what methods of self-protection they have. Many would suddenly drop off the leaf and disappear, for example.

Interviewer: I believe you were asked to take photographs of caterpillars.

Laura: Yes. That was fun. When they heard I was into photography, two of the scientists asked me to help. They'd found some rare caterpillars, which had only ever been seen in Colombia before, and they wanted to see what kind of butterflies these species would turn into. For their research, they wanted pictures of the caterpillars in different positions – curled up, stretched out, crawling across leaves, munching away at something. It was very interesting.

Interviewer: You must've learned a lot about caterpillars.

Laura: Yes, although the researchers said they still don't know much about caterpillars – and we need to know more. Some species cause major problems for farmers. In Costa Rica, for example, where they grow lots of fruit, caterpillars often invade and destroy it. The more scientists discover, the better they will be at preventing that happening. What's even more crucial, though, is that caterpillars are food for other animals like birds and bats. Also, butterflies, which caterpillars turn into, help plants produce fruit.

Interviewer: Did you travel around the jungle much?

Laura: We went on a few trips. I'll never forget one long hike. There was a storm and everything got incredibly muddy, and our guide kept warning us about poisonous snakes. I'm usually pretty calm, but when I got attacked by some mosquitoes and then fell over in a stream, I got very upset and said I wanted to give up. We kept going, though. <u>I can see I was being rather ridiculous and I wish I hadn't reacted in that way.</u> I suppose you can learn from experiences like that, and I'd probably cope better if I ever had that sort of adventure again.

Interviewer: Has your time in Costa Rica affected your ideas about what you'll do in the future?

Laura: Well, I was really lucky to travel to such an amazing place. I don't know if I'll ever get the chance to go somewhere like that again, but it's changed me. I used to think of insects like caterpillars as just annoying really, but now I can see how important they are in nature and how they need to be respected. <u>And watching the researchers there made me realise that a university degree in biology is something that'd suit me when I finish school.</u>

Interviewer: Thank you Laura. That was very interesting.

[pause]

Now you will hear Part Four again.

tone

[The recording is repeated.]

[pause]

That is the end of Part Four.

There will now be a pause of five minutes for you to copy your answers onto the separate answer sheet. Be sure to follow the numbering of all the questions. I shall remind you when there is one minute left, so that you are sure to finish in time.

[pause – four minutes]

You have one more minute left.

[pause – one minute]

That is the end of the test. Please stop now. Your supervisor will now collect all the question papers and answer sheets.

Test 2 answer key

Reading and Use of English

Answer key with extra explanations in Resource bank

Part 1

1 D **2** A **3** C **4** A **5** C **6** B **7** B **8** D

Part 2

9 order **10** to **11** has **12** part **13** be
14 Whilst/While/Although/Though **15** only **16** well

Part 3

17 inexperienced **18** survival **19** permission **20** independence
21 adventurous **22** consideration **23** Unfortunately **24** memorable

Part 4

25 ADVISED me | to watch
26 have predicted | SUCH a
27 is / 's rude | to USE
28 UNLESS you | (have/'ve) put
29 to have | RUN out of
30 was no/was not any/wasn't any | SIGN of

Part 5

31 B **32** D **33** C **34** D **35** B **36** C

Part 6

37 G **38** D **39** A **40** C **41** E **42** F

Part 7

43 C **44** A **45** D **46** B **47** A **48** B **49** A **50** B **51** C **52** D

Listening

Answer key with extra explanations in Resource bank

Part 1

1 B **2** A **3** B **4** C **5** B **6** A **7** B **8** C

Part 2

9 extreme sports **10** Deep Drop **11** (small) rivers
12 torch **13** dinosaur **14** back **15** flooding
16 safety kit **17** narrow entrance **18** (tiny) insects

Part 3

19 H **20** F **21** C **22** E **23** B

Part 4

24 A **25** C **26** A **27** C **28** B **29** C **30** B

Audioscript

Test Two.

I am going to give you the instructions for this test. I shall introduce each part of the test and give you time to look at the questions. At the start of each piece you will hear this sound:

tone

You will hear each piece twice.

Remember, while you are listening, write your answers on the question paper. You will have five minutes at the end of the test to copy your answers onto the separate answer sheet.

There will now be a pause. Please ask any questions now, because you must not speak during the test.

[pause]

Now open your question paper and look at Part One.

[pause]

PART 1 *You will hear people talking in eight different situations. For questions 1 to 8, choose the best answer (A, B or C).*

Question 1 *You hear a girl telling a friend about a family trip she went on to a climbing centre.*

[pause]

tone

Boy: How was your climbing centre trip?

Girl: Well, we hadn't studied the brochures very carefully so we weren't sure what to expect – we thought we'd enjoy being surprised when we got there. There was an enormous tower to climb up and then swing down! It did look fun, but it was much bigger than I thought it'd be and I didn't fancy trying it. Everyone else in my family loved it though – <u>in fact, it eventually developed into them all seeing who could be the best at everything. I really wasn't keen on that.</u> Luckily there were some smaller climbing walls too, so I had a go at those.

Boy: Ah, right.

[pause]

tone

[The recording is repeated.]

[pause]

Question 2 *You hear a teacher talking to her class about a visit to a science exhibition.*

[pause]

tone

Woman: As you know, we're off to the science exhibition next week, the theme of which is fire and light. There'll be demonstrations throughout the day, so we'll check the programme of events to see which ones will be the most interesting – educationally I mean. For example, there's one on what a candle needs in order to keep burning, which we covered in class last week, <u>so take your notes to look at, then write down any additional observations.</u> There's also a display about what happens to light when it hits different objects – hopefully you'll recall that from the homework you were asked to do. Any questions?

[pause]

tone

[The recording is repeated.]

[pause]

Question 3 *You hear two students discussing a film they saw on TV.*

[pause]

tone

Boy: Did you see that film on TV last night? The one about a girl who was adopted by the politician and his wife.

Girl: Yeah I did, it was unusual and I liked that. It was a bit weird in places, though. <u>I never imagined the girl would have such an impact on the couple who adopted her.</u>

Boy: <u>Or that her adoptive parents would behave the way they did in the end.</u> I thought the actor who played the girl was brilliant. But I wasn't convinced the director made a wise decision about the actors who played the parents.

Girl: They're both famous though, so you can understand why he did it.

[pause]

tone

[The recording is repeated.]

[pause]

Question 4 *You hear a woman talking about her work as a fashion designer.*

[pause]

tone

Woman: <u>The first piece of clothing I remember altering was a vest I wore in high school. We had a dress code which we had to follow, but I disliked the fact that everybody looked more or less the same. I used to sew things onto my clothing so I was still following the rules about what you could wear at school, but managed to look slightly different.</u> So many people just want to fit in these days, for obvious reasons. But I believe we're all starting to dress in similar ways. My clothes allow people to express parts of their personality that they haven't necessarily shown before, and so their unique character can be revealed.

[pause]

tone

[The recording is repeated.]

[pause]

Question 5 *You hear a student talking about a project he has done on bees.*

[pause]

tone

Boy: I'd like to tell you about a very unusual kind of bee that's found in parts of North and Central America. It's one of several types of nesting bee, which lay their eggs beneath the ground and then head out to search for nectar. This process usually takes place in environments with plenty of flowers, to ensure a reliable supply of food. However, a colony has now been found in the ashes of an active volcano. The area is known for temperatures which can get as high as 42 degrees centigrade. You really wonder how the bees manage to live in this inhospitable place, where little other life is found.

[pause]

tone

[The recording is repeated.]

[pause]

Question 6 *You hear a girl talking about giving up social media for two weeks.*

[pause]

tone

Girl: I took part in a class research project. I had to give up social media for two whole weeks. I imagined I'd find it far too challenging – I certainly didn't think my ability to concentrate would improve so much. Of course, there were moments when it would've been easy to give in to temptation and sneak a look at my phone. After all, no one was checking up on me. And it was obvious nobody believed me when I said I didn't cope too badly without social media, but I didn't care. So I read news websites instead, and realised how much I could learn from them. I've stuck with them ever since.

[pause]

tone

[The recording is repeated.]

[pause]

Question 7 *You hear a teacher telling his students about some research into learning and memory.*

[pause]

tone

Man: Let me tell you about some recent psychological research. You might find it useful. So, the psychologists gave students a list of words for easy-to-draw objects such as 'apple' or 'balloon'. After the researcher called out each word, some students had to write it repeatedly, while others were asked to sketch a picture to represent it. Then the students were given an additional unrelated task while background music was played. After that, the students had 60 seconds to write down all the words they could come up with from the first assignment. <u>Those who'd illustrated the words did a much better job of remembering them than those who'd written them multiple times.</u>

[pause]

tone

[The recording is repeated.]

[pause]

Question 8 *You hear a girl talking about the choir she sings in.*

[pause]

tone

Girl: I'm a member of a choir and, recently, we performed at the city university – an amazing event. It was to mark the fact that the main building was actually 500 years old. <u>And, for the first time ever, we got to sing with an adult choir – very scary, but we were inspired by the example they set, and I was amazed that they actually make a living out of doing it.</u> We were nervous we wouldn't understand their music director's instructions, but we'd had several practice classes with him beforehand. He wasn't particularly impressed with our singing, actually, but apparently we did alright on the day.

[pause]

tone

[The recording is repeated.]

[pause]

That is the end of Part One.

Now turn to Part Two.

[pause]

PART 2

You will hear a girl called Kelly talking about an activity called potholing, which involves exploring underground caves. For questions 9 to 18, complete the sentences with a word or short phrase.

You now have forty-five seconds to look at Part Two.

[pause]

tone

My name's Kelly Johnson and I'm going to talk about potholing – that's basically going underground to explore caves. My uncle got me into this unusual activity. A lot of people who explore caves want to study the geology of them, or even the history – because thousands of years ago people lived in them. <u>But he actually took up this activity because he's enthusiastic about extreme sports and potholing was just one of many things he tried.</u>

I live in an area where there are lots of caves so there's plenty of choice for people who love potholing. Everyone wants to visit the Peak Cavern, which is, I think, the largest cave in the area. For my first attempt, I wanted to go to one with the name Dragon Cave – because it sounded cool. <u>In the end, my uncle decided we'd go to one known as Deep Drop, because the conditions there are perfect for beginners.</u>

Inside the cave it was a whole new world. <u>When we got down there, we discovered small rivers running through – I thought that was amazing, and we decided to follow one.</u> In fact a lot of caves have surprising things like that. I've heard of people coming across waterfalls. It's even possible to find underground lakes too.

We had to have the right equipment before setting off on that first potholing trip. A helmet was obviously essential, <u>and we each had a torch with us but mine didn't work properly.</u> It wasn't a big deal though, because I wasn't leading the way or anything. And we wore waterproof clothing because you can get very wet when you're inside caves.

The rocks underground can be stunningly beautiful. And my imagination really got to work. <u>I remember going past a rock formation that was very similar in shape to a dinosaur and I pointed it out to my uncle.</u> Later he drew my attention to some rocks he'd spotted that looked like a sculpture of a bear. Really cool!

It's hard work exploring underground and people get very tired. For this reason my first trip wasn't too long. Even so, my uncle managed to cut his knee – it was really sore actually. <u>I hit my back on a rock and had a good moan about that, but it was really hurting me.</u> And the next day I noticed I'd bruised my arm a bit too – nothing serious though!

Professional potholers say going into caves can be a bit risky. There are falling rocks to look out for, and slippery surfaces that people need to be careful walking on. <u>Flooding is what makes the experts most nervous</u>, but they say you're fine if you check the conditions beforehand.

People going underground have to take different things with them depending on the cave they're exploring – a ladder, for example to help them climb down rock faces or diving gear if they have to go underwater. <u>And nobody could possibly go down there without a safety kit</u> – it should have everything in it that you might need in an emergency.

I enjoyed going with my uncle so much that we went on a second trip together, <u>to a cave which had a narrow entrance so it was really difficult for us to squeeze our way inside.</u> On that same trip we came across a tiny tunnel – too small for us to crawl into, but we could see light at the end of it, which was frustrating.

Since then I've done lots of potholing trips and they've all been brilliant. Once I was in a cave full of what my team leader said were fossils that were 600 million years old. <u>And on another trip I was exploring a cave where there were thousands of tiny insects, which were glowing in the dark</u> – it was so beautiful. That's a moment that really stands out for me. And I'm going to keep exploring caves whenever I can.

[pause]

Now you will hear Part Two again.

tone

[The recording is repeated.]

[pause]

That is the end of Part Two.

Now turn to Part Three.

[pause]

PART 3

You will hear five short extracts in which teenagers are talking about a journey they recently went on. For questions 19 to 23, choose from the list (A to H) what each speaker says about the experience. Use the letters only once. There are three extra letters which you do not need to use.

You now have thirty seconds to look at Part Three.

[pause]

tone

Speaker 1

Last summer I went to visit relatives in Australia. It was my first long flight on my own and I was nervous. Everyone kept telling me what I should and shouldn't do: drink lots of water, move around, things like that. I didn't do any of it because I got really comfortable in my seat and I fell asleep, but I was fine. Another time I'd borrow my Dad's camera though. I thought mine would be good enough but I was wrong about that. I could've got some fantastic shots of the city at night when we came into land if I'd had something better with me.

[pause]

Speaker 2

Last year I went on a school trip by ferry to some islands in the North Sea. The crossing was incredibly rough and one of my friends got ill – I felt really sorry for her. I'd actually forgotten to bring the seasickness tablets my mum had got for me – she was annoyed about that – but anyway I felt perfectly okay and actually it was a great experience. I also enjoyed meeting some Spanish students on the boat. I'd been learning the language and it was cool trying it out. We said we'd keep in touch – they're coming to the UK next year. I haven't heard from them yet, but hopefully we'll meet up again.

[pause]

Speaker 3

I went on a journey with my grandparents earlier this year. Before we set off Dad said I should look after them as they're getting older now, but I didn't have to do much, just carry grandma's luggage for her, which wasn't a problem at all. It started badly when we rolled up at the airport thinking our flight was leaving at seven. Grandad's always telling us to get to the airport early – advice my parents never seem to follow – but it was a good job we did listen this time as it turned out the flight was at six. We just made it. If we hadn't, we'd have missed a fantastic holiday.

[pause]

Speaker 4

I really enjoyed a coach tour I went on with my class last spring. It was to see some historic buildings in the north of the country. It was hot on the coach and there was no leg room. My friends complained about that but I didn't think it was too bad. We had an awesome guide who pointed out the different architecture and told us about how incredibly skilful builders were centuries ago. And it helped me make up my mind about what to do after leaving school. I realised architecture's what I want to study. My parents were really surprised when I told them. But they agree it's a good plan.

[pause]

Speaker 5

[pause]

The trouble with flying is there's so much queuing and sitting around on hard seats at airports. And I'm often fed up because I always seem to lose something there. So I never look forward to it. Last year I went to stay with an uncle in the USA. He'd been ill and Mum thought I could take care of him as well as having a holiday. <u>Anyway, on the plane there I was sitting next to a girl about my age and we got talking. Before I knew it we'd arrived. She was so interesting that I forgot about the annoying stuff.</u> I wish I'd kept in touch with her really!

[pause]

Now you will hear Part Three again.

tone

[The recording is repeated.]

[pause]

That is the end of Part Three.

Now turn to Part Four.

[pause]

PART 4

You will hear an interview with a school student from Scotland, called Jake Dawson, who is talking about cycling in the snow in a town in Finland. For questions 24 to 30, choose the best answer (A, B or C).

You now have one minute to look at Part Four.

[pause]

tone

Interviewer: Today I'm with sixteen year old school student Jake Dawson, from Scotland, who's just spent part of the winter with relatives in Finland. Jake, welcome! Did you find Finland very different from Scotland?

Jake: Well, one thing about where I was in northern Finland was that it was dark during the day, and although it isn't always bright sunshine in Scotland in the winter months, that did take some getting used to. The public buildings reminded me of where I come from in Scotland, though – something really impressive about their style. And the streets were always full of activity – the weather didn't seem to put people off, which is hardly the case in my hometown.

Interviewer: Do you go out in the snow in Scotland?

Jake: It's not that I don't go out in snowy weather in Scotland, but I travel around an awful lot by car when I'm there – I did in Finland too. But instead of complaining as I usually do back home, I was able to take in the stunning landscape, and see just how much the snow was a part of that. When I go out in the snow in Scotland, it's a case of having to, for studying and things, not for enjoyment.

Interviewer: And in Finland, you cycled in the snow, which you hadn't done before.

Jake: Yes, back home it's not something people do when it snows! The number of cyclists really thins out then. But to deal with the ice on the roads and make sure you're safe, what you really need is a mountain bike with thick tyres and good brakes – that isn't too difficult to get hold of actually. The thing is we all just assume the temperature's so low that we'll freeze. But in Finland they just carry on as normal.

Interviewer: What made cycling in the snow in Finland special?

Jake: Well, it'd be going too far to say drivers kept out of our way and made allowances for us, but they were never actually aggressive. Getting around in the snow was less tricky than at home, though – there was definitely more done to make sure routes for cyclists could be used at all times – although I did take a deep breath when I had to deal with some of the major crossroads – I'd have been grateful for underpasses for cyclists to use.

Interviewer: And didn't you cycle across a frozen river?

Jake: Yes! It was so cold that the ice was really thick. Some people were lowering their bikes down the bank and cycling across – they obviously thought it was safe – my cousin thought so too. I was pretty reluctant to follow him, but knew I'd never have another chance to do it. So I set off – but then part of the way there I just had to turn back. It looked really dark under that ice!

Interviewer: Did you ever have any accidents while you were cycling in the snow?

Jake: Well, I'd been warned that it's really easy to lose your sense of direction in the snow and I'd been told to pay extra attention to road signs, and also to concentrate on not sliding out of control and letting the bike slip out from under me. But one time that's exactly what happened because I got too sure of myself. Another cyclist behind me had to brake sharply and then actually ran into me. We were both okay, but it was pretty embarrassing!

Interviewer: I can imagine! And were you still keen to cycle when you got back to Scotland?

Jake: Sure! In Finland, I'd been taught that in snow, you should keep your weight back, stay relaxed and not speed, so I made up my mind to carry on doing that back home. I'd recently bought a top-of-the-range bike so at least I know how to ride it properly in bad weather. Some of the guys I go to college with are thinking about starting to cycle there next term to save money, so it might be good to do that.

Interviewer: Well, thanks, Jake for …

[pause]

Now you will hear Part Four again.

tone

[The recording is repeated.]

[pause]

That is the end of Part Four.

There will now be a pause of five minutes for you to copy your answers onto the separate answer sheet. Be sure to follow the numbering of all the questions. I shall remind you when there is one minute left, so that you are sure to finish in time.

[pause – four minutes]

You have one more minute left.

[pause – one minute]

That is the end of the test. Please stop now. Your supervisor will now collect all the question papers and answer sheets.

Test 3 answer key

Reading and Use of English

Answer key with extra explanations in Resource bank

Part 1

1 C **2** A **3** D **4** B **5** B **6** A **7** C **8** B

Part 2

9 who **10** up **11** what **12** it/this/that **13** such **14** are
15 making **16** from/with

Part 3

17 unacceptable **18** demanding **19** appearance **20** Consequently
21 imperfect **22** inspiration **23** successfully **24** intention

Part 4

25 it IMPOSSIBLE | to
26 MUST have/'ve | eaten
27 is/'s BEING | shown
28 have to/need to BELIEVE | what I
29 far as | I am/I'm CONCERNED
30 has/'s been | an INCREASE

Part 5

31 D **32** B **33** A **34** C **35** B **36** A

Part 6

37 D **38** G **39** A **40** F **41** C **42** E

Part 7

43 C **44** D **45** A **46** B **47** D **48** A **49** B **50** D **51** A **52** C

Listening

Answer key with extra explanations in Resource bank

Part 1

1 C **2** A **3** A **4** C **5** C **6** B **7** A **8** A

Part 2

9 history **10** passengers **11** (physical) fitness
12 watch **13** privacy **14** heights **15** playing cards
16 festival **17** stars **18** warm

Part 3

19 H **20** D **21** A **22** G **23** E

Part 4

24 C **25** B **26** B **27** A **28** C **29** B **30** A

Audioscript

Test Three.

I am going to give you the instructions for this test. I shall introduce each part of the test and give you time to look at the questions. At the start of each piece you will hear this sound:

tone

You will hear each piece twice.

Remember, while you are listening, write your answers on the question paper. You will have five minutes at the end of the test to copy your answers onto the separate answer sheet.

There will now be a pause. Please ask any questions now, because you must not speak during the test.

[pause]

Now open your question paper and look at Part One.

[pause]

PART 1 *You will hear people talking in eight different situations. For questions 1 to 8, choose the best answer (A, B or C).*

Question 1 *You hear a girl talking about making online videos.*

[pause]

tone

Girl: I've always loved watching videos online and that inspired me to make them myself. My idea was to make videos giving advice on fashion, and I did listen to the feedback I got – not necessarily positive – from the people who watched them. I didn't have a particular audience in mind, it was just a fun hobby and I had no big ambitions. Luckily, I had the chance to learn through trial and error. The camera I used wasn't that sophisticated, and I made my films in the evening using a desk light, but you've got to start somewhere! Mastering videos requires patience but I got there by just sticking at it.

[pause]

tone

[The recording is repeated.]

[pause]

Question 2 *You hear a girl talking about some photos her dad has taken.*

[pause]

tone

Boy: What are these, Kate?

Girl: Oh, they're just a collection of photos that Dad took of me over a 10-year period – he's an amateur photographer.

Boy: Really? They're great! Is he intending to put them up somewhere or something?

Girl: Well, they may well end up in an exhibition, I suppose. But these are really about looking back over what he's done so he can chart his progress, because he's hoping to be good enough to turn professional one day.

Boy: Still, they're a great way of preserving the past, aren't they?

Girl: Yeah, and I think he's actually enjoyed looking back at special moments in our family life.

Boy: I can understand that.

[pause]

tone

[The recording is repeated.]

[pause]

Question 3 *You hear a young man talking about being an inventor.*

[pause]

tone

Man: I invented a smart phone app that gives the location of school buses on a map, and indicates whether you're on the bus and what time you'll be home. People ask me how I come up with new ideas. Well, it's true that many young inventors study websites featuring the latest trends in technology, and I'm sure doing that can generate ideas. Noticing people's frustrations and problems with their everyday routine, you know identifying practical things that need fixing, is another approach though, and that works for me. Some people are born original and imaginative and can get inspiration out of thin air. But I can't seem to do that.

[pause]

tone

[The recording is repeated.]

[pause]

Question 4 *You hear a teacher giving a talk to her class about bats.*

[pause]

tone

Woman: Today we're studying bats – did you know there are around 1,300 species in the world! And most of them fly at night – but how do they manage that without crashing into things – or each other? Well, one called a tube-nosed bat, for example, uses its long nose to make a high whistling call at night to detect things like food sources around it, and to prevent collisions. And another, the greater bulldog bat, can catch fish in open water! It sends out sound waves – by making a high-pitched call – and then detects when those sound waves hit an object, such as a fish! … Okay, now let's see some photographs of …

[pause]

tone

[The recording is repeated.]

[pause]

Question 5 *You hear a boy talking about going to take part in an archaeology project in Italy.*

[pause]

tone

Boy: I'm off to Italy soon – to help out on a site where my dad's working as an archaeologist, excavating an old city. Apparently it was once a really amazing place, but then the whole area was mysteriously abandoned. It'd be cool to be there helping when they finally find out why! So I'm keen to go. And actually, Dad's uncovered some evidence that our ancestors originated from there, so he thinks it'd be a real chance for me to learn more about them. I guess he's right – although Dad also thinks I might want to do archaeology myself one day – we'll have to see about that.

[pause]

tone

[The recording is repeated.]

[pause]

Question 6 *You hear a guide at a science museum talking about a new virtual-reality device that visitors can try.*

[pause]

tone

Man: You're probably wondering what this is that I'm holding! Well, it's a virtual-reality headset that allows you to see the world exactly how different creatures see it. So you'll get an insight into how trees and plants might look to different forest animals. You can decide which creature you'd like to be, and that determines which views you'll get – you might be swooping over the treetops, for example, or running around on the ground! And you'll be amazed to find that, according to scientists, many creatures don't see the same colours as we do, so the images of the forest you're in will be totally different from what you might expect.

[pause]

tone

[The recording is repeated.]

[pause]

Question 7 *You hear two students talking about some research on listening to music while studying.*

[pause]

tone

Boy: I read some research that said listening to music when you're studying helps concentration – a strange subject for research!

Girl: No stranger than other research that scientists do. I think it'd be quite useful. What did it say?

Boy: <u>That instrumental music is better than songs when you're studying – not surprising – you can really be put off if you start singing along.</u>

Girl: <u>Because with songs, you're bound to want to understand what the artist's saying, which is distracting.</u>

Boy: I like listening to upbeat music when I'm studying, though. It makes me study much longer than I normally would.

Girl: If I'm enjoying the music too much when I should be working, then it's anything but helpful.

[pause]

tone

[The recording is repeated.]

[pause]

Question 8 *You hear a radio presenter talking about something that happens in space.*

[pause]

tone

Man: Here's some exciting news for people living in the northern hemisphere and especially people interested in space — today marks the emergence of the black moon. That may sound scary but it's just the name given to the second new moon in a month. <u>As you may or may not know, a new moon occurs when the lunar orbit is between the Earth and the sun. Therefore, the side of the moon lit by the sun is facing away from our planet, making it virtually invisible to the naked eye. It's actually a very rare occurrence. The last black moon was over two years ago, and the next one won't occur for several years.</u>

[pause]

tone

[The recording is repeated.]

[pause]

That is the end of Part One.

Now turn to Part Two.

[pause]

PART 2

You will hear a girl called Alison giving a class presentation about a holiday she had on a traditional sailing ship. For questions 9 to 18, complete the sentences with a word or short phrase.

You now have forty-five seconds to look at Part Two.

[pause]

tone

Last summer, I spent two weeks on a tall ship, travelling round parts of Europe. Tall ships are traditional sailing boats – they're made of wood and have tall masts and large sails. Nowadays, they're used for adventure holidays and teaching sailing skills. I was lucky to be sponsored by an educational charity which was set up to support teenagers who like history – the idea is that helping them take part in certain traditional activities is a good way to do this.

My first day on the ship was spent in port, preparing for the voyage. The ship had fourteen permanent crew members and thirty so-called trainees, who were people like me. The captain gave an introductory speech and I was surprised to hear that there were mainly teenagers on the ship, that nobody, apart from him, was over thirty-five, and that most trainees were between fifteen and eighteen. He also stressed that there could be no passengers on board, meaning that everyone was expected to work.

I already knew I'd be working – I wanted to, in fact. But I must admit, I seriously wondered whether my physical fitness would be up to it. It turned out to be okay actually, and I coped in situations which needed a lot of self-discipline – just having to get up incredibly early, for example.

The trainees were divided into teams and each team worked for four hours at a time – from eight a.m. to twelve, and then another four-hour stretch from eight p.m. till midnight. Every couple of days, we'd get a different shift, as it'd be called on land – it's known as a watch when you're out at sea.

Like most trainees I found it quite difficult to adapt to the timetable – in fact, no one got any sleep at first. Lots of things about being on the ship were new for us – like not having internet access, which was really tough. What I found more challenging than anything, though, was there was no such thing as privacy. For example, I had to share a small cabin with five other people.

But, generally, we all got on well. The work we did varied – we cleaned things, helped in a kitchen, and even took control of the wheel, steering the ship sometimes. That made me very nervous, actually – imagine making mistakes with that! Another thing I did was climb the twenty-metre main mast to help fix something. I've always been terrified of heights and I'm proud I managed to do that.

It wasn't all work, of course. We went swimming a lot, which was good fun, and it was nice just hanging out with the other trainees, you know, just chatting – we needed that time to relax. Playing cards was the main thing we did when we weren't on duty, though.

We stopped at different ports occasionally. We could get off the ship and do things like sightseeing or shopping. There was a market in France, for instance, that many trainees thought was brilliant – I didn't go there because I spent time on a beautiful beach instead – I wouldn't have wanted to miss that. We had a great day in Barcelona too, though unfortunately we arrived just too late to catch the festival that had taken place there.

But mostly, we were out at sea, and although we worked a lot, we still saw some amazing things – like hundreds of dolphins and flying fish. So many of the sunsets at sea are impressive too, <u>and I hadn't been prepared for just how many stars are visible at night</u> – there's no light pollution, of course.

If any of you fancy going on a tall ship, I could give you details of websites to look at, and also some useful tips. You must have waterproof clothes, for example. I didn't take many, but luckily our ship had a good supply of them. <u>I was short of warm jumpers and trousers too, which was annoying because I had to borrow some from another girl.</u>

I'd definitely recommend going on a tall ship if you get the chance.

[pause]

Now you will hear Part Two again.

tone

[The recording is repeated.]

[pause]

That is the end of Part Two.

Now turn to Part Three.

[pause]

PART 3

You will hear five short extracts in which teenagers are talking about making a new friend. For questions 19 to 23, choose from the list (A to H) what each speaker says. Use the letters only once. There are three extra letters which you do not need to use.

You now have thirty seconds to look at Part Three.

[pause]

tone

Speaker 1

I made a new friend last week. I was just on the bus to school when this girl sat down next to me and asked if I could tell her which stop to get off at for the City Museum. We got chatting. It turned out she'd come from Canada to visit elderly relatives. It seemed to me that she was a bit lonely so I invited her to come along to a concert at my school that evening. We found out we were both into the same kind of music and were so busy chatting about all the bands we liked that I almost forgot to tell her to get off.

[pause]

Speaker 2

I've known the kid who lives next door since forever, although we didn't really get on too well. But when we were about eight, his father took us to swimming lessons on Saturday mornings. We both struggled at first because we were so scared of the water, but that kind of brought us together and we've been best mates ever since. That's probably because we've found we share lots of interests. He's cleverer than me but that's never really been a problem for either of us. Mum says the way he talks – you know like he's much older than he really is – reminds her of my cousin. I'm not sure about that.

[pause]

Speaker 3

Anna's definitely my closest friend. We've shared lots of good and bad moments over the last few years. I broke my wrist last term, for example, and Anna helped me loads, carrying my schoolbooks, that sort of stuff. We were in the same class at school and I remember thinking when I met her that she looked a bit boring, so I wasn't too friendly and I tried to avoid her. I soon realised, though, that she was just shy and actually it turned out that she's got a great sense of humour. She and her family are moving into our street soon so we're going to be neighbours, which'll be great.

[pause]

Speaker 4

Eric's a really interesting person. I got to know him through a project which involved teenagers in different countries working on producing a website together. He was living in Ireland then. He seemed a really nice guy and I wasn't disappointed when we eventually got together face-to-face. The strange thing is, his dad ended up being offered a job in the town where I live so now we're actually going to the same school. Eric found it quite hard moving to a new place and he missed his school back in Ireland, so I'm sure it helped a lot that he already had something in common with me and my mates.

[pause]

Speaker 5

[pause]

I started at a new school last year. It was exciting but also very scary to be going somewhere five times the size of my old school. So it was reassuring to find myself sitting next to someone I thought I knew – a girl I'd seen visiting my neighbours. We got talking and it turned out she'd never actually been anywhere near our street – the two of them just looked similar. Anyway, we've become really good friends. We both love horseriding and taking photos, and we're both planning to study medicine. I'm sure we'll never lose touch whatever we end up doing.

[pause]

Now you will hear Part Three again.

tone

[The recording is repeated.]

[pause]

That is the end of Part Three.

Now turn to Part Four.

[pause]

PART 4

You will hear an interview with a young man called Oliver Stanford, who is talking about how he became a professional gardener. For questions 24 to 30, choose the best answer (A, B or C).

You now have one minute to look at Part Four.

[pause]

tone

Interviewer: Today I'm with Oliver Stanford, a gardener in a big gardening company. Oliver, gardening's becoming popular with young people, isn't it? How did you get interested?

Oliver: Well, when I was younger, we lived in the countryside. Mum works as an interior designer and particularly enjoyed doing up the inside of the house – which always looked fantastic! The same couldn't be said about the outside, though! That never got much attention – and it wasn't until I started going to friends' houses, with beautiful gardens, that I saw how awful ours looked in comparison! So I talked to my parents and managed to persuade them to help me set about tidying it up.

Interviewer: And you decided to become a professional gardener.

Oliver: Yeah, but getting there wasn't straightforward. My parents offered to provide the money for me to go to university – to study horticulture – I didn't take them up on it. I wasn't convinced doing a full-time degree was right for me. I felt I needed hands-on work experience as well, so I worked as an assistant gardener, while studying for my degree part-time. But I'd underestimated how much effort I'd need to put in – loads of assignments! I got there in the end!

Interviewer: And after graduating, you got your first full-time job at a garden centre.

Oliver: Yes – it was really tough! I started in the winter, outside in freezing glasshouses, putting seeds into pots full of wet soil! My parents had to persuade me not to give up. But I was hoping the experience would help prepare me for the kind of work that lay ahead. Planting seeds then, some time later, selling the fully grown plants, ready to go into someone's garden, gave me great satisfaction.

Interviewer: And you knew you'd make a successful gardener. Where did that confidence come from?

Oliver: Well, I could see that some gardeners didn't really have the in-depth knowledge of plants that I was building up. And I'm aware of what time of year to do things – what can be left for later and what has to be done now – keeping on top of all that is something I've got used to and am now good at – some gardeners find that difficult, and you won't be any good at the job if you can't do that. So what I want to move on to next is designing gardens that people really appreciate.

Interviewer: And now you're working with a firm of city gardeners – very different from what you're used to.

Oliver: Yes, the clients are different too! Many seem to have the idea that we can create the perfect garden in just a week, although my boss always refuses to accept their deadlines – and once they understand why, they're fine about it. I did think we'd have problems with access to clients' gardens, you know, because we need to move quite large machinery in there for some jobs we do. I haven't had any issues with that, though.

Interviewer: Are there any jobs you haven't liked doing?

Oliver: There was one. The house owners were completely changing their garden. The grass had already been taken up and big stones put down, which I didn't think were suitable. Then they asked us to get rid of some hedges that had grown right round the garden. I wasn't keen because they were a habitat for birds and other creatures. Anyway, we did it, but there wasn't much that we could plant instead, as the soil there was such poor quality.

Interviewer: But you really love the work, don't you?

Oliver: Yes – it's great to work outside with other gardeners, even if they're not as into getting their hands dirty and growing stuff as I am! The real appeal for me is that we can arrive in a garden, which is completely overgrown, and we leave it looking spectacular. I'm actually looking forward to getting a flat with a small garden myself – my salary isn't quite sufficient to stretch to that at the moment – but I'm sure that'll change!

Interviewer: I'm sure it will! Thanks, Oliver.

[pause]

Now you will hear Part Four again.

tone

[The recording is repeated.]

[pause]

That is the end of Part Four.

There will now be a pause of five minutes for you to copy your answers onto the separate answer sheet. Be sure to follow the numbering of all the questions. I shall remind you when there is one minute left, so that you are sure to finish in time.

[pause – four minutes]

You have one more minute left.

[pause – one minute]

That is the end of the test. Please stop now. Your supervisor will now collect all the question papers and answer sheets.

Test 4 answer key

Reading and Use of English

Answer key with extra explanations in Resource bank

Part 1

1 C **2** B **3** A **4** B **5** C **6** B **7** D **8** D

Part 2

9 what **10** it **11** does **12** enough **13** have/need
14 long **15** a **16** how

Part 3

17 extension **18** heavily **19** harmful **20** development
21 irrelevant **22** temptation **23** evidence **24** unreasonable

Part 4

25 TAKE up | all (of)
26 ASKED me | not to tell
27 were | in FAVOUR of
28 PUT me | off
29 should not/shouldn't have/'ve | BROUGHT up
30 is/'s/was SUCH | a good/great film/movie

Part 5

31 C **32** A **33** D **34** D **35** B **36** C

Part 6

37 E **38** B **39** G **40** A **41** F **42** D

Part 7

43 B **44** C **45** A **46** B **47** D **48** B **49** D **50** A **51** B **52** C

Listening

Answer key with extra explanations in Resource bank

Part 1

1 A **2** B **3** C **4** C **5** A **6** C **7** C **8** B

Part 2

9 wood **10** winter **11** cousin **12** In Flight **13** dinosaur
14 920 / nine hundred and twenty **15** sound(s) **16** bird table
17 bread **18** telescope

Part 3

19 B **20** F **21** H **22** D **23** A

Part 4

24 B **25** C **26** B **27** A **28** A **29** B **30** C

Audioscript

Test Four.

I am going to give you the instructions for this test. I shall introduce each part of the test and give you time to look at the questions. At the start of each piece you will hear this sound:

tone

You will hear each piece twice.

Remember, while you are listening, write your answers on the question paper. You will have five minutes at the end of the test to copy your answers onto the separate answer sheet.

There will now be a pause. Please ask any questions now, because you must not speak during the test.

[pause]

Now open your question paper and look at Part One.

[pause]

PART 1 *You will hear people talking in eight different situations. For questions 1 to 8, choose the best answer (A, B or C).*

Question 1 *You hear a music teacher talking to members of a school choir.*

[pause]

tone

Woman: Okay, I think today's practice went quite well, but remember that the concert is only two weeks away and you could sound a lot better. We've been practising these songs for over a month now, and I've told you to learn them off by heart – which you've done. Each of you needs to be aware of how your voice fits in with the overall sound, and my feeling today was that you're more sensitive towards each other than you were. <u>What needs to come across is the feeling that you're putting everything into these songs. They currently sound quite flat, so there's still work to do there.</u>

[pause]

tone

[The recording is repeated.]

[pause]

Question 2 *You hear two friends discussing a presentation given by a writer.*

[pause]

tone

Boy: Did you enjoy yesterday's presentation?

Girl: Well, I don't know that writer's work, but I love doing creative writing – it was interesting to hear about some of the things she does to help her develop her stories ...

Boy: Like how she listens to people's conversations to get the language right.

Girl: Yeah, but she doesn't include teenage slang – that's really difficult for someone older to do well. <u>I was impressed at how much effort she makes to get to know real people who she then puts into her books – I'd always imagined writers spend their lives on their laptops trying to work out how their imaginary characters will think and act.</u>

Boy: Yeah, me too.

[pause]

tone

[The recording is repeated.]

[pause]

Question 3		*You hear a girl talking about a cycle race she took part in.*
		[pause]
		tone
	Girl:	I enjoy competitive cycling on off-road tracks, and I've won several races, so it's hardly surprising that everyone just thought I'd win again. In fact, I didn't – I came second – and that was down to me underestimating how muddy the route was going to be. Afterwards, some people criticised me, for being too sure I'd win. Okay – it's true that I'm always quite sure of myself in races – I never assume I can't be beaten though. And I don't have regrets about the amount of practice I did beforehand, because I'd done what I generally do, and any more would've been too much – well that's what I think anyway.
		[pause]
		tone
		[The recording is repeated.]
		[pause]
Question 4		*You hear a radio item about an art competition in South Korea.*
		[pause]
		tone
	Man:	The streets of Seoul in South Korea are usually full of activity. But that changes during the extremely wet monsoon season, which keeps people indoors. However, a recent art competition aimed to change this. Artists were encouraged to paint large pieces of artwork, called murals, in different places round the city. The only problem? They had to use hydrochromic paint – only visible when it comes into contact with water. So, to see the paintings, residents had to go outside during the wet weather. The artists who came up with the idea won two of the world's most important prizes, though it's unclear whether residents responded well to this unusual way of creating interest in art.
		[pause]
		tone
		[The recording is repeated.]
		[pause]

Question 5 *You hear two friends talking about a teenage boy who won a surfing competition.*

[pause]

tone

Girl: That TV programme last night about the surfing competition was amazing, wasn't it? I mean, what makes someone decide to enter a competition like that when they're only seventeen!

Boy: Well not many kids like us get that sort of opportunity. I wish I had the chance to do something like that.

Girl: And I'd be really proud if I'd managed to beat all those adults and win – it was strange he didn't seem that bothered about it.

Boy: I thought he'd be making much more of it than he did. But it was certainly a brave thing for him to do.

Girl: Some people don't see the dangers though, do they?

[pause]

tone

[The recording is repeated.]

[pause]

Question 6 *You hear a man talking about a problem some turtles had trying to reach a wildlife park in Japan.*

[pause]

tone

Man: Every summer, hundreds of turtles crawl to a popular Japanese wildlife park from the nearby ocean in order to find food and shelter. Unfortunately, in the past, some turtles used to get caught between railway tracks which run between the ocean and the park. The turtles were unable to find a safe way out in any direction, so park officials and railway engineers got together to dig small U-shaped ditches close to the tracks to provide safe places for the creatures to remain in until they were found. Since then, railway workers have rescued ten turtles and delivered them safely to their new home in the wildlife park.

[pause]

tone

[The recording is repeated.]

[pause]

Question 7 *You hear a teacher telling his class about an 'environment day' the school is having.*

[pause]

tone

Man: You all know the school is doing something to mark environment day next month. This is a day when we all think more carefully about environmental issues and about improving our local environment. In other years we've acted on suggestions you've come up with, like picking up litter from the school grounds, and teachers have also asked you to spend time checking websites for detailed information on endangered species and their habitats. These are interesting and worthwhile things to do. <u>What we're looking for this time, though, is to do some long-term good, for example by planting trees.</u> So if any of you would like to volunteer to ...

[pause]

tone

[The recording is repeated.]

[pause]

Question 8 *You hear a man talking about an extreme marathon he took part in.*

[pause]

tone

Man: Last spring I competed, in the US, in what's called an ultra-marathon. It's a one-hundred-and-sixty kilometre race that only one thousand one hundred people have ever attempted – of those only fourteen have actually managed to complete the course. These statistics don't make you feel too confident as you set off, I can tell you! The route itself is extraordinarily demanding – the unmarked, rocky tracks are dangerous and running at altitude's tough – completing the race has been compared to climbing Mount Everest twice! <u>Then there's the fact that no medical help is provided and there are only two water-filling stations along the route. That's what did it for me in the end.</u>

[pause]

tone

[The recording is repeated.]

[pause]

That is the end of Part One.

Now turn to Part Two.

[pause]

PART 2

You will hear a boy called Jake giving a class presentation about birdwatching, which is his hobby. For questions 9 to 18, complete the sentences with a word or short phrase.

You now have forty-five seconds to look at Part Two.

[pause]

tone

I'd like to tell you about my hobby – birdwatching – which I do with my dad. Our favourite place is a lake called Bellewater, which is great for birds but it's a bit far for us to get there too often. We also go to a wood nearer home – we went there last week actually – and a hillside we like is also a place we go to from time to time.

People in the UK generally start birdwatching early in the morning because that's when birds are most active. Actually, there aren't many birds to see right now because it's autumn and many summer visitors have already flown south. The winter is when you get the greatest number and variety here, because birds from Arctic regions come for the warmer climate at that time of year. Birdwatchers also like the spring – that's when all the young birds are hatching.

Many birdwatchers keep records of the birds they see, the dates, locations and so on. I used to write everything in a notebook – basically, I got the idea from my dad – he got me into birdwatching. Then, my cousin sent me a link to a birdwatcher's blog and suggested I try something similar. So I did, and it's been great – loads of people read my blog, even my mum!

There's a sort of birdwatchers' network online and we post links to other blogs we like – I have a link to Red Wing, which is written by a girl called Maisie, and she features a link to In Flight – that's mine. And we both list a link to another blog called Long Feathers, and so on.

The blog was great for a trip we did to Australia. The wildlife there's amazing – not just the birds but other animals too – like the kangaroo, for example. We spotted one huge bird called a cassowary, with a long blue neck and a kind of horn on top of its head – it looked like some sort of dinosaur. There's a photo of it on my blog.

In Australia, I spotted about fifty different birds I'd never seen before. Birdwatchers often keep a count of the types of birds they've seen. The world record-holder's observed over eight thousand different species. I'm currently at nine hundred and twenty, and if I keep going, I should get to five thousand by the time I'm my dad's age – and he's at three thousand two hundred so far!

I like birdwatching for various reasons, though – not just to see lots of them. It's fascinating to observe bird behaviour, for example – like the way they fly together in groups. And there are things I'd love to learn more about. For instance, I often can't distinguish between birds from different sounds they make, though I'm not bad when it comes to identifying differences in their appearance.

You don't have to travel a long way to see birds. We actually get several different types in our garden – having some trees helps. And because I really wanted to study birds in more detail, I made a bird box so that they could build their nests there – I did that a while back. And, not long ago, me and my dad managed to build a bird table and put food on it for them, which really meant I could see them close up.

I used to put out bread for them but apparently that's not a great idea because it contains things that aren't good for birds. Fat, which you can sometimes buy in small balls especially for them, is popular and won't do them any harm. They'll go for various seeds and nuts too, of course.

If you're interested in doing some birdwatching, there are a few things it's good to have. To identify birds you'll need a good reference guide – or you can get an app for this. You'll need a pair of binoculars to see birds properly, and <u>keen birdwatchers often have a telescope. Dad's actually trying to find me one that isn't too expensive and I'm really looking forward to using it when he does.</u> The other thing to have is a good camera. I borrow my dad's actually.

OK, that's all, but if you have any other questions see me after the class.

[pause]

Now you will hear Part Two again.

tone

[The recording is repeated.]

[pause]

That is the end of Part Two.

Now turn to Part Three.

[pause]

PART 3

You will hear five short extracts in which members of a dance class are talking about preparing to take part in a dance show. For questions 19 to 23, choose from the list (A to H) what each speaker says about their experience. Use the letters only once. There are three extra letters which you do not need to use.

You now have thirty seconds to look at Part Three.

[pause]

tone

Speaker 1

I learnt so much from rehearsals. People were always giving advice, like how to deal with aching legs and painful feet. I'd heard all that before though – but we certainly needed some energy! My dance teacher made me rehearse constantly to get everything as good as it could be – I even started dreaming about the dances I had to learn. There were sessions where we were told to make up our own dances. We really had to think hard about that but everyone came up with some great moves. That brought us together and made us cooperate with each other and share our ideas. Without that, we'd never have done so well!

[pause]

Speaker 2

We had a lot of routines to learn, but that wasn't a problem because we practised all day every day with a teacher who was really strict with us and made sure we kept focussed and remembered everything we had to do! Anyway, by the time we got to the show, my body was already aching from all those rehearsals! And then the show was so popular that we were told we had to do five extra performances. That kind of thing happens a lot, apparently, so I just learnt to rise to the challenge like everyone else. And it all went really well – we all agreed it felt great when we'd done it!

[pause]

Speaker 3

They warned us younger dancers that we might really suffer with aching bodies after our first major rehearsal but actually, unlike other people in my dance group, it wasn't an issue for me. And as the rehearsals went on, we all began to get excited about the show. But I started to feel I wasn't up to everyone else's level. Then, at one workshop, we had to teach each other some dance moves we knew – we hadn't been told that this was going to happen. Anyway, no one apart from me knew anything about breakdancing and they were really pleased to learn. Even the teacher seemed impressed by what I could do, which felt good!

[pause]

Speaker 4

During rehearsals, everyone was always talking about how they felt – you know – mainly anything they were unhappy about. I found that a bit unhelpful actually – I'm not the sort of person who's comfortable talking about my problems. Anyway, as the final performance approached, we kept running through our routines to make them as near perfect as we could and I found that, as long as I concentrated, it was easy enough to learn my part and so I started to relax about it all. On the night, we all did our best and our teacher seemed to be really pleased with what we'd managed to achieve.

[pause]

Speaker 5

[pause]

During rehearsals, we were suddenly moved to a bigger dance space to get more of a feel of how it would be to perform on stage. We spent hours going over every tiny detail of the performance, which was hard work and very repetitive – it started to make me nervous that we were never going to get things right. But in the end it all started to come together. In fact, my dance director made me believe anything was possible if I was determined enough, and I danced better than I ever would've imagined I could. And the show was a great success.

[pause]

Now you will hear Part Three again.

tone

[The recording is repeated.]

[pause]

That is the end of Part Three.

Now turn to Part Four.

[pause]

PART 4

You will hear an interview with a teenager called Tina Barker, who is talking about a local archaeology project she took part in last summer. For questions 24 to 30, choose the best answer (A, B or C).

You now have one minute to look at Part Four.

[pause]

tone

Interviewer: Today I'm with Tina Barker, who's been volunteering at a summer community archaeology project which aims to trace the history of her village. But it took time to get started, didn't it Tina?

Tina: Yes, the idea came from local people who wanted to find out more about the village's history. They settled on the field we're digging in now as a starting point, because an archaeologist came and found evidence that the village had once extended out there. He actually set up the project and looked for volunteers. He stressed to us that it was really important to get suitable tools – so that we didn't destroy things, I guess! Some of the stuff we needed was quite specific to the job we were doing, so it was a while before we tracked it down. But in the meantime, the current owners of the land were impressed by his proposal, and it didn't take them long to decide we could go ahead.

Interviewer: So what's the group trying to find out?

Tina: Well, the area we're digging in has never been used for growing crops, so it's been undisturbed for centuries. We think underneath we'll find old roads, and the foundations of a 500-year-old building that we believe was in the area, though we're not too sure what the purpose of it was! The real mystery for me is why the entire population just left the area at one point, for no apparent reason. So I've been helping to look for clues in the village births and deaths records – like being a detective, really!

Interviewer: And you've found something yourself, haven't you?

Tina: Yes, a silver wedding ring. The archaeologist on site thought it was over a hundred years old – but not worth a lot. Anyway, what appealed to me about it was imagining how the woman who lost it must have felt – because it must've meant a lot to her. My mum lost her wedding ring in the park last year, and was really upset. We never found it – but I imagine someone looking in a hundred years' time might dig it up. Who knows, maybe they'll even start looking into who its owner was.

Interviewer: So there's always an archaeologist on site then?

Tina: Yes, he's great. He's explained how much we can learn from just the tiniest bits of pottery, and how important it is to preserve them. But he'd soon shout at people if he thought they were messing around – I certainly wouldn't want to be shown up like that. And he'd order people off the site if they didn't follow his instructions. But we do try not to cause any damage.

Interviewer: But I've heard there are cows in the area that could actually do some damage?

Tina: Mmm, most mornings we'll find the cows have knocked down the temporary fence that's been erected, so they're always wandering into the excavation area – they'll walk all over everything in one part of the site and we don't notice till it's too late because we're busy working in another. They seem genuinely curious about what's going on, but the archaeologist says we'll have to fill everything in again if they carry on, and that'd be a real pity.

Interviewer: But hopefully that won't happen … So what have you got out of the project?

Tina: Well, everybody agrees it's great to spend time sifting through the soil in detail, knowing you might just discover something about ordinary people living in our village in the past – it makes you forget all your own problems, cos you're so focused on that. And I never saw much point in taking my time over things … seeing something in the soil, say, and then working carefully around it ... that was a challenge at the outset. I never thought I'd adapt to it like I have.

Interviewer: And the group have found lots of interesting items. Will they be sold?

Tina: Well, I guess that could get us some money to help us continue! Actually, it'd be great if all these items could stay where they were found so that future residents could find out what life was like in their village, but the archaeologist says most of the stuff will eventually go off to big museums, for everyone to appreciate … Anyway, it's been a great summer!

Interviewer: Thanks, Tina!

[pause]

Now you will hear Part Four again.

tone

[The recording is repeated.]

[pause]

That is the end of Part Four.

There will now be a pause of five minutes for you to copy your answers onto the separate answer sheet. Be sure to follow the numbering of all the questions. I shall remind you when there is one minute left, so that you are sure to finish in time.

[pause – four minutes]

You have one more minute left.

[pause – one minute]

That is the end of the test. Please stop now. Your supervisor will now collect all the question papers and answer sheets.

35159

OFFICE USE ONLY - DO NOT WRITE OR MAKE ANY MARK ABOVE THIS LINE — Page 1 of 2

Cambridge Assessment English

Candidate Name		Candidate Number	
Centre Name		Centre Number	
Examination Title		Examination Details	
Candidate Signature		Assessment Date	

Supervisor: If the candidate is ABSENT or has WITHDRAWN shade here ○

First for Schools Reading and Use of English Candidate Answer Sheet

Instructions

Use a PENCIL (B or HB).

Rub out any answer you want to change using an eraser.

Parts 1, 5, 6 and 7:
Mark ONE letter for each question.

For example, if you think A is the right answer to the question, mark your answer sheet like this: 0 A B C

Parts 2, 3 and 4: Write your answer clearly in CAPITAL LETTERS.

For parts 2 and 3, write one letter in each box. 0 EXAMPLE

Part 1

	A	B	C	D
1	○	○	○	○
2	○	○	○	○
3	○	○	○	○
4	○	○	○	○
5	○	○	○	○
6	○	○	○	○
7	○	○	○	○
8	○	○	○	○

Part 2

		Do not write below here
9		9 1 ○ 0 ○
10		10 1 ○ 0 ○
11		11 1 ○ 0 ○
12		12 1 ○ 0 ○
13		13 1 ○ 0 ○
14		14 1 ○ 0 ○
15		15 1 ○ 0 ○
16		16 1 ○ 0 ○

Continues over →

OFFICE USE ONLY - DO NOT WRITE OR MAKE ANY MARK BELOW THIS LINE — Page 1 of 2

35159

SAMPLE

© Cambridge Assessment 2021 Photocopiable

35159

OFFICE USE ONLY - DO NOT WRITE OR MAKE ANY MARK ABOVE THIS LINE

Page 2 of 2

Part 3		Do not write below here
17		17 1 0 ○ ○
18		18 1 0 ○ ○
19		19 1 0 ○ ○
20		20 1 0 ○ ○
21		21 1 0 ○ ○
22		22 1 0 ○ ○
23		23 1 0 ○ ○
24		24 1 0 ○ ○

Part 4		Do not write below here
25		25 2 1 0 ○○○
26		26 2 1 0 ○○○
27		27 2 1 0 ○○○
28		28 2 1 0 ○○○
29		29 2 1 0 ○○○
30		30 2 1 0 ○○○

Part 5				
31	A ○	B ○	C ○	D ○
32	A ○	B ○	C ○	D ○
33	A ○	B ○	C ○	D ○
34	A ○	B ○	C ○	D ○
35	A ○	B ○	C ○	D ○
36	A ○	B ○	C ○	D ○

Part 6							
37	A ○	B ○	C ○	D ○	E ○	F ○	G ○
38	A ○	B ○	C ○	D ○	E ○	F ○	G ○
39	A ○	B ○	C ○	D ○	E ○	F ○	G ○
40	A ○	B ○	C ○	D ○	E ○	F ○	G ○
41	A ○	B ○	C ○	D ○	E ○	F ○	G ○
42	A ○	B ○	C ○	D ○	E ○	F ○	G ○

Part 7						
43	A ○	B ○	C ○	D ○	E ○	F ○
44	A ○	B ○	C ○	D ○	E ○	F ○
45	A ○	B ○	C ○	D ○	E ○	F ○
46	A ○	B ○	C ○	D ○	E ○	F ○
47	A ○	B ○	C ○	D ○	E ○	F ○
48	A ○	B ○	C ○	D ○	E ○	F ○
49	A ○	B ○	C ○	D ○	E ○	F ○
50	A ○	B ○	C ○	D ○	E ○	F ○
51	A ○	B ○	C ○	D ○	E ○	F ○
52	A ○	B ○	C ○	D ○	E ○	F ○

OFFICE USE ONLY - DO NOT WRITE OR MAKE ANY MARK BELOW THIS LINE

Page 2 of 2

35159

SAMPLE

© Cambridge Assessment 2021 Photocopiable

36863

OFFICE USE ONLY - DO NOT WRITE OR MAKE ANY MARK ABOVE THIS LINE

Cambridge Assessment English

Candidate Name		**Candidate Number**	
Centre Name		**Centre Number**	
Examination Title		**Examination Details**	
Candidate Signature		**Assessment Date**	

Supervisor: If the candidate is ABSENT or has WITHDRAWN shade here ○

First for Schools Listening Candidate Answer Sheet

Instructions

Use a PENCIL (B or HB).

Rub out any answer you want to change using an eraser.

Parts 1, 3 and 4:

Mark ONE letter for each question.

For example, if you think **A** is the right answer to the question, mark your answer sheet like this:

Part 2:

Write your answer clearly in CAPITAL LETTERS.

Write one letter or number in each box.
If the answer has more than one word, leave one box empty between words.

For example:

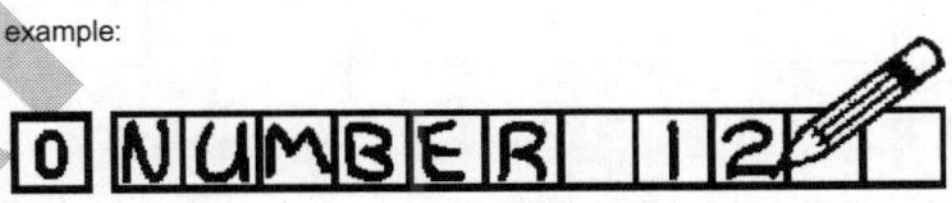

Turn this sheet over to start.

SAMPLE

OFFICE USE ONLY - DO NOT WRITE OR MAKE ANY MARK BELOW THIS LINE

36863

© Cambridge Assessment 2021 Photocopiable

36863

OFFICE USE ONLY - DO NOT WRITE OR MAKE ANY MARK ABOVE THIS LINE

Page 2 of 2

Part 1

1	A ○	B ○	C ○	5	A ○	B ○	C ○
2	A ○	B ○	C ○	6	A ○	B ○	C ○
3	A ○	B ○	C ○	7	A ○	B ○	C ○
4	A ○	B ○	C ○	8	A ○	B ○	C ○

Part 2 (Remember to write in CAPITAL LETTERS or numbers)

		Do not write below here
9		9 1 ○ 0 ○
10		10 1 ○ 0 ○
11		11 1 ○ 0 ○
12		12 1 ○ 0 ○
13		13 1 ○ 0 ○
14		14 1 ○ 0 ○
15		15 1 ○ 0 ○
16		16 1 ○ 0 ○
17		17 1 ○ 0 ○
18		18 1 ○ 0 ○

Part 3

19	A ○	B ○	C ○	D ○	E ○	F ○	G ○	H ○
20	A ○	B ○	C ○	D ○	E ○	F ○	G ○	H ○
21	A ○	B ○	C ○	D ○	E ○	F ○	G ○	H ○
22	A ○	B ○	C ○	D ○	E ○	F ○	G ○	H ○
23	A ○	B ○	C ○	D ○	E ○	F ○	G ○	H ○

Part 4

24	A ○	B ○	C ○
25	A ○	B ○	C ○
26	A ○	B ○	C ○
27	A ○	B ○	C ○
28	A ○	B ○	C ○
29	A ○	B ○	C ○
30	A ○	B ○	C ○

OFFICE USE ONLY - DO NOT WRITE OR MAKE ANY MARK BELOW THIS LINE

Page 2 of 2

36863

SAMPLE

© Cambridge Assessment 2021 Photocopiable

Part One Answer
You must write within the grey lines.

SAMPLE

© Cambridge Assessment 2021 Photocopiable

Part Two Answer You must write within the grey lines.	
Write your question number here:	

SAMPLE

© Cambridge Assessment 2021 Photocopiable

Acknowledgements

The authors and publishers acknowledge the following sources of copyright material and are grateful for the permissions granted. While every effort has been made, it has not always been possible to identify the sources of all the material used, or to trace all copyright holders. If any omissions are brought to our notice, we will be happy to include the appropriate acknowledgements on reprinting and in the next update to the digital edition, as applicable.

Key: RUE = Reading and Use of English, ST = Speaking Test

Text

RUE1: Elsevier Ltd. for the adapted text from *Construction and Building Materials, Vol. 115,* Arul Arulrajah et al., Strength assessment of spent coffee grounds-geopolymer cement utilizing slag and fly ash precursors, pp. 565–575, Copyright © 2016, with permission from Elsevier via the Copyright Clearance Center; The Guardian for the adapted text from 'My foolish leap of faith' by Tom Robbins, *The Guardian,* 15.02.2009. Copyright © 2020 Guardian News & Media Ltd. Reproduced with permission; DOGOMedia Inc. for the adapted text from 'Computer-generated Rembrandt Painting unveiled in Amsterdam' by Kim Bussing, DOGOMedia Inc., 09.05.2016. Copyright © 2016 DOGOMedia Inc. Reproduced with permission; The Guardian for the adapted text from 'How physical exercise makes your brain work better' by Ben Martynoga, *The Guardian,* 15.06.2016. Copyright © 2020 Guardian News & Media Ltd. Reproduced with permission; **RUE2:** DOGOMedia Inc. for the adapted text from 'Winter Activities that go beyond Skiing and Snowboarding' by Kim Bussing, DOGOMedia Inc., 31.01.2016. Copyright © 2016 DOGOMedia Inc. Reproduced with permission; The Independent for the adapted text from 'What the future may hold for rollercoasters, according to the people who design them' by Kashmira Gander, *The Independent,* 20.07.2016. Copyright © The Independent. Reproduced with permission; ABC for the adapted text from 'Do trees communicate with each other?' Anna Salleh with guests Dr Suzanne Simard, Professor Ian Anderson and Professor Hans Lambers © 2015 ABC. Reproduced by permission of the Australian Broadcasting Corporation – Library Sales; **RUE4:** University of Dundee for the adapted text from 'Slower melting ice cream in pipeline, thanks to new ingredient' by Roddy Isles, University of Dundee, 31.08.2015. Copyright © University of Dundee. Reproduced with kind permission; The Guardian for the adapted text from 'Eye-opening research suggests sleeping crocodiles still keep watch' by Oliver Milman, *The Guardian,* 21.10.2015. Copyright © 2020 Guardian News & Media Ltd. Reproduced with permission.

Photography

The following images have been sourced from Getty Images.

ST1: PhotoAlto/Frederic Cirou/Brand X Pictures; Manuela/Cultura; Juice Images RF; **ST2:** Robert Kneschke/EyeEm; Smith Photographers; The Washington Post; Sandy Huffaker/Corbis News; **ST3:** Troy Aossey/Taxi; davidf/E+; PHIL MOORE/AFP; NurPhoto; **ST4:** SolStock/E+; Hans Neleman/Stone; Â© Hello Lovely/Corbis; skynesher/E+.

Audio

Audio production by dsound recording studios.

Typesetting

Typeset by QBS Learning.

Visual materials for the Speaking test

Why have the friends decided to do these things together?

1A

1B

Why might it be important for the students to listen carefully in these lessons?

1C

1D

1E

Should teenagers spend their summer holidays away from home, doing activities with other young people?

- **having new experiences**
- **learning to be independent**
- **not being with family**
- **missing friends**
- **meeting new people**

What are the people enjoying about eating in these places?

2A

2B

What might the people find difficult about these new activities?

2C

2D

2E

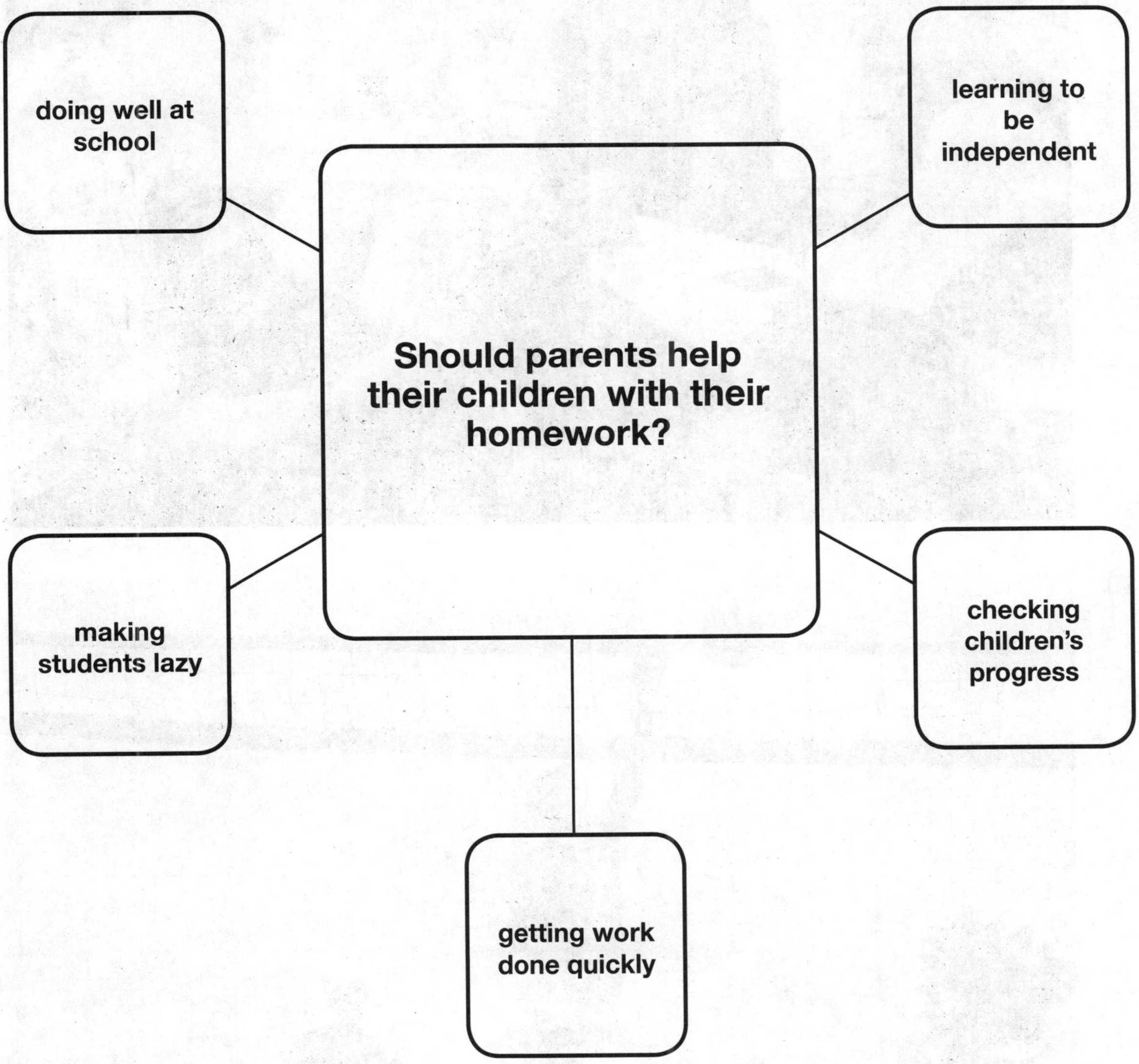
Should parents help their children with their homework?
doing well at school
learning to be independent
making students lazy
checking children's progress
getting work done quickly

Why are the people watching their friends in these situations?

3A

3B

What are the people enjoying about doing these things on a summer afternoon?

3C

3D

3E

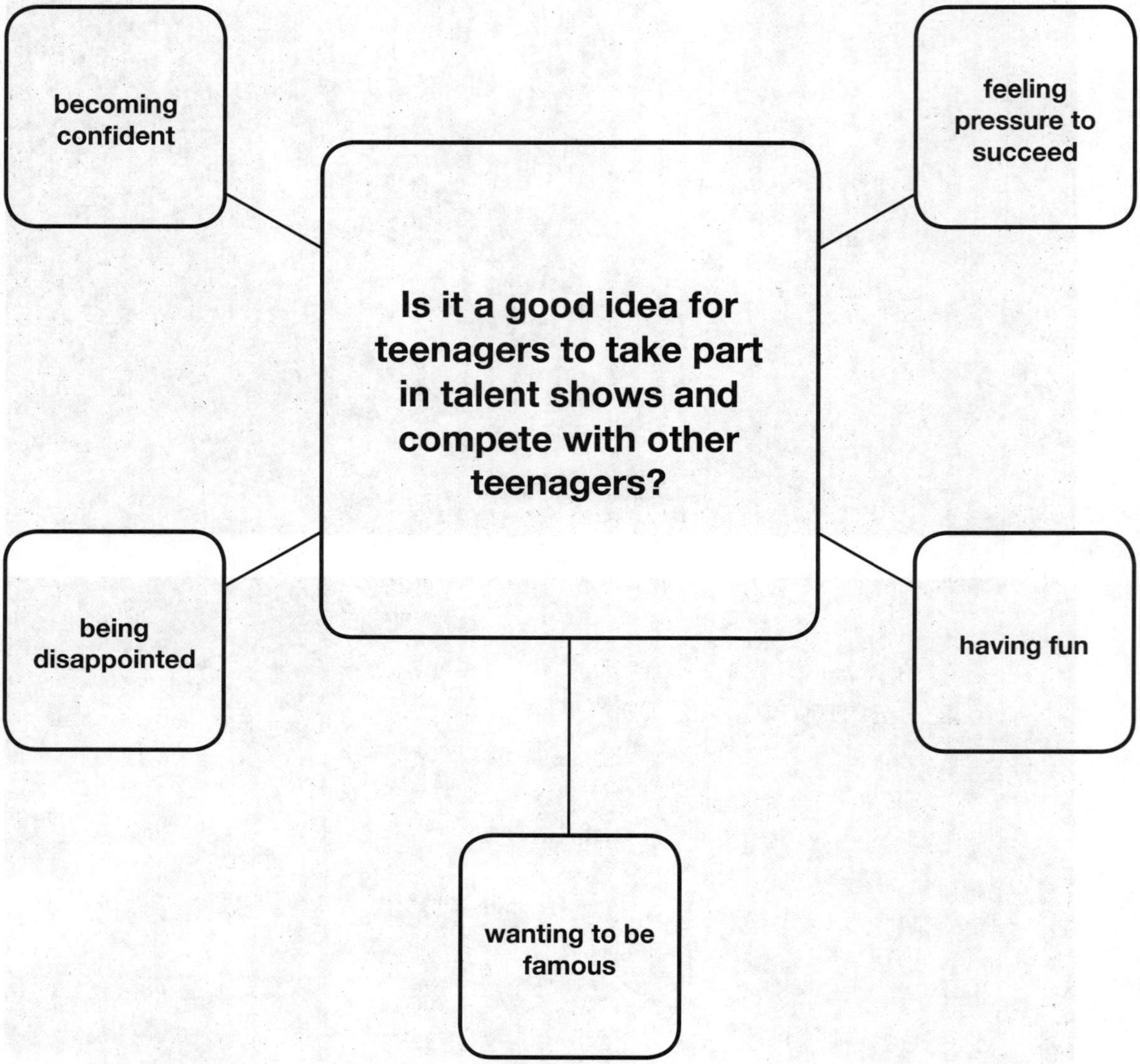
becoming confident
feeling pressure to succeed
Is it a good idea for teenagers to take part in talent shows and compete with other teenagers?
being disappointed
having fun
wanting to be famous

What are the people enjoying about taking part in these competitions?

4A

4B

What might the people find difficult about practising these things?

4C

4D

4E

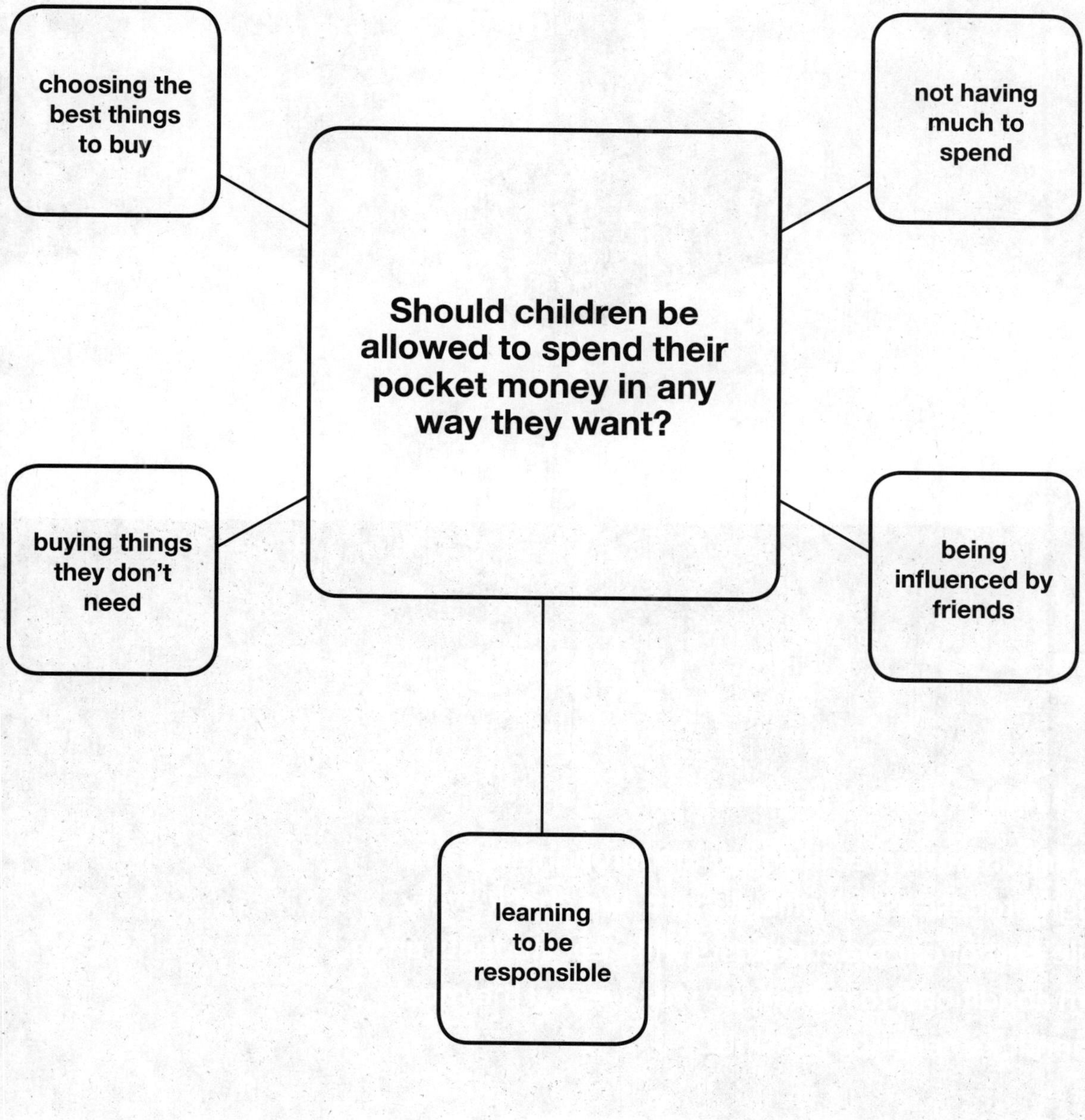
Should children be allowed to spend their pocket money in any way they want?
choosing the best things to buy
not having much to spend
buying things they don't need
being influenced by friends
learning to be responsible

Caiaimage/Sam Edwards/Gett

SPOT THE DIFFERENCE

That's right – there is no difference.

All our authentic practice tests go through the same design process as the official exam. We check every single part of our practice tests with real students under exam conditions, to make sure we give you the most authentic experience possible.

The official practice tests from Cambridge.